DON'T KEEP ME SILENT:
One Woman's Escape
from the Chains of Islam

by Mina Nevisa

Copyright © Mina Nevisa, 1999

ISBN: 0-9674744-0-X

To contact publisher:
Don't Keep Me Silent
PO Box 4331
Silver Spring, MD 20914-4331

Book design:
PRINT PARTNERS
1-877-262-2300 • www.printpartners.net

DEDICATION

This book is dedicated to those servants in Christ who serve the Lord in silence and humility, to those who have ever devoted their lives to spread the good news of salvation, and to those who have been called by the Lord and through his anointing have led thousands of lost souls to our living God, Jesus Christ. I dedicate all my trials and experiences to those who have been persecuted for their faith. Let those persecutions be a shining candle among all people.

I am truly indebted and very grateful to my very dear brothers and sisters who contributed their personal efforts and scholarship to assist in publishing this book. May the Lord bestow his abundance richly in your lives through his miraculous ways.

CONTENTS

CONTENTS

FOREWORD

I cannot give up but want every day to be more available for the Lord to use me in his wonderful and marvelous ways.

After my last journey from Iran, having passed through the ups and downs of the storms of life, I cast my anchor, rolled up my sails, put away my oars, let go of the rudder and ran to my Lord. I have thrown myself into the arms of my Lord and feel the firmness and security of the Lord in my steps.

PREFACE

It was four o'clock in the morning when the phone rang. On the phone a woman's cries were heard—the cries of someone who had just heard the good news of Christ the night before. Mahin was a 53-year-old woman who had come to Sweden to visit her only son for the last time. She had advanced breast cancer and had been informed by the doctors that she would die in less than 6 months.

Mahin had given her heart to Christ the night before, leaving her life completely in the Lord's hands. She had confessed that she wanted to live with Jesus Christ the rest of her life—whether it was be six months or six days. During that early morning call, she kept crying on the phone and it was hard to understand what she was saying.

My husband and I rushed to her place and found her sitting on the floor in the middle of the livingroom, bowing down with her hands lifted up and eyes full of tears. She was praising the Lord with all her heart and her being, repeating over and over, "The Lord has healed me. The Lord has healed me."

The previous night, when she had accepted Christ as her savior, she had had a dream. In that dream Jesus had come beside her bed and put his hands on her, telling her that from that very moment she was free from cancer and any kind of disease. Mahin was very touched, but also very confused, so she asked, "Are you

Jesus or Muhammed?" Jesus answered, "I am the one who has the power to heal."

Mahin was healed of cancer from that night by the majestic power of Jesus Christ. Many churches have been blessed since then by Mahin's testimony about how Christ healed her.

When Mahin returned to Iran, her whole family came to the Lord. Even the two doctors who examined her and found no trace of cancer in her body came to Christ. She has since started a secret prayer group in her home with family and a few friends, including the two doctors.

Witnessing so many wonders of my Lord, all the spiritual experiences I have had in him, and the leading of the Holy Spirit have been the most important reasons why the idea of writing this book was born in my heart.

The book you have in your hand represents my total spiritual experiences since 1983 when I gave my heart totally to Jesus Christ forever. It is a book that presents all those Islamic and cultural traditions that rule fundamentalist Muslims, and it shows how much Islamic culture affects the daily lives of Muslims socially and politically. It will help the reader understand the world of Islam and realize what kind of feelings and spiritual transitions a fanatic Muslim faces when deciding to convert from Islam to Christianity.

There are great values and admirable social teachings in some areas of Islam, and I still admire these. But I intend to describe that it is not enough to have faith and be holy; rather, it is necessary to perceive the character of God, his relationship with mankind, and his divinity.

My commitment to God has allowed me to write down what he has done in my life in overcoming the forces that threatened to endanger my life. I have read many times this verse written by Paul and it has become my favorite: "For God did not give us a spirit of timidity, but a spirit of power, of love and of self-discipline." (2 Timothy 1:7)

Jesus Christ is the one who promised much more than empty slogans for the difficulties and calamities facing mankind today. My Lord is the one who fulfilled what he promised and fulfilled whatever had been prophecied. What you read in this book is not an exaggeration. It is the reality of God's promises that whoever submits his life to the hands of the Lord will experience the fulfillment of the promises.

It has always been my desire to be one of those who go and not one of those who remain. I have always wanted to face reality, and God has shown me his reality through his wonders and his permanent presence in my life. Anyone who opens his heart and eyes to the Lord Jesus Christ will actually see how he turns the impossibles to possibles in this life. Without Christ, however, there will be no joy in going and no peace in staying.

Today I sing the Lord's songs—not only without any sorrow—but also overfilled with joy. There is no sunset in my life anymore, only sunrise where the patient and quiet heart of my life continues its beating. I hear the great and wonderful voice of God who calls his son to him.

Today there is nothing remaining from what afflicted my life and filled my soul with anguish. The whispers of my sorrows have gone away from me forever.

After many long years of darkness, my day has arrived full of the Lord's rest. I am born again. I prefer to die rather than to live without Christ. I do not mind any more praising and worshipping the name of the Lord in an empty place on the ground. I never again want to put myself and my soul in front of dead prophets or in rusty chains of the law that were nothing but punishment for me. I never again want to be kept silent.

The ways of the Lord lead neither to the right nor to the left, but his ways lead to the inside of a man's heart. It is only there where the name of the Lord can remain forever and from which his divine peace and rest flow on everything.

"Salvation is found in no one else; for there is no other name under heaven given to men by which we must be saved." (Acts 4:12)

I have taken great pains in publishing this book in an effort to promote understanding among those who urgently seek establishment of their faith and a trusting relationship with God. This book is also written for those believers who sincerely desire to deepen their faith and so produce more and more fruit for the kingdom of God.

DON'T KEEP ME SILENT:

One Woman's Escape from the Chains of Islam

TEHERAN, MY MEMORABLE TOWN

Every time I think about my childhood, I remember the beautiful living room that we had in our house. The sun always shone through the big window which was in the livingroom, no matter which season of the year it was. Through that window we could see part of the garden and street. I remember how jealous I was when children started to go to school in the beginning of fall, and I had to stay at home and watch them through that favorite window.

It was a beautiful afternoon and the sun was shining through my favorite window. My father was sitting in his special armchair and was reading his Koran. He had his glasses on and seemed very tired. He used to do the same thing, sit and read, every single day when he came back from work. He lived completely in his own world.

When he was reading the Koran, he never heard when anyone spoke to him; and if he heard, he never answered. Right after finishing reading the Koran, he took two different newspapers and read. My mother made tea which was especially prepared on a *samavar* for him. My father loved drinking tea in the evening. He always drank two cups which were brought to him one after the other. He was actually a very sweet man with a nice smile on his face, especially while reading his Koran. He was a very kind man whose religion had made him quite serious and hard.

I remember times that my mother stared at him for a few minutes, took a deep breath, and shook her head. I never really understood what she meant by shaking her head like that and what she thought of my father. Was she wondering how lucky she was for marrying such a religious man like my father? Or was she wondering how heavy the atmosphere of her life was? I wish I understood what she meant by shaking her head like that.

I was born into a fundamentalist Muslim family in Teheran, the capital of Iran, which is a populous city in the northwest of Iran with almost fifteen million people. Iran means "land of the Aryans." The marvelous mountain of Alborz, the mines of gold and silver, the oil wells, and all the artistic treasures have made this country special and unique.

I come from a big, wealthy, fundamentalist Muslim family where I was the youngest child (before, of course, I was rejected for my Christian faith). My mother always used to say that although she had six children before my birth, she was so happy and excited to have one more baby girl at home.

I was proud of having a family with four brothers and two sisters. My mother was constantly busy with the housework, but she was very organized. Discipline ruled all the aspects of life in our house.

My father was a teacher of the Koran and Islamic theology at the University of Teheran and a Persian-Arabic translator. He also owned a factory, but he was not there much since he was busy with all the work in the university. Even without his constant attention, the factory workers worked exactly as they were ordered, and my father was satisfied. They cut leather the size that my father specified and crafted with nails and hammers the way that he instructed. My father followed the same system at home with his family, everything exactly the way that he desired.

My father was a kind and hardworking dictator who always said that hard work is part of a Muslim's life and belief. Joy, sorrow, wife, children and the whole of life were treasured as long as they did not trespass his religious belief in the *Shariat* (the rules and laws of Islam.)

My grandfather was a fundamentalist high priest and a great writer who wrote more than fifteen books on Islamic topics. He also taught Koranic theology at the Feizieh Theology School in the holy city of Qum. In this school students study the Koran and Islamic law. Then, according to their grades and studies, they can reach different levels of *Rohaniat* which means Islamic clergy, the society of Mullahs (Islamic priests). In that school after the students graduate, they become Mullahs and Imams at different levels.

By the time my grandfather was seventy years old, he was quite famous and respected by everybody. My grandmother had passed away many years before my grandfather. Her death made my grandfather much older and more tired, but he never remarried. He always said that he wanted to remain faithful to his wife.

After my grandmother's death, my parents asked my grandfather to move in and live with us. I remember that I used to sit on my grandfather's knees, and he told me Koranic stories. I was never allowed to listen to any story that was not explained by my father or my grandfather. I loved my grandfather very much, and we had a very close relationship. He was actually my best friend, and I told him anything that I had in my heart.

In Iran unity of the family is very important. When parents get old and sick, they still have full respect and love from their children. We were all very proud of my grandfather since he was so sweet and so well known.

When my grandfather turned eighty years old, he became

sick and had problems with his heart and his sight. He had been quite healthy before then. Heart and eye problems did not allow him to read and write properly anymore. He had serious problems with his eyes, and doctors said that he must have an operation. For a man who had read and written almost all his life, it was the saddest thing that could have happened to him. In spite of this, he was still invited to give some Islamic lectures; but most of the time he stayed at home. Even the doctor would come to our house to attend to him.

I felt intense pain in my heart and cried every single time that I saw his health failing. I thought that I would die if something happened to my grandfather. My mother would hug me and say that everything would be all right. She promised that my grandfather would get better soon, but that was nothing but a dream. He got worse and worse every day.

One extremely cold winter night my grandfather seemed tired, very tired. His attitude completely changed. He wanted to meet the whole family, even the relatives. He visited everybody and spoke his last words with them.

It was the month of Ramadan, and although he was so sick and weak, he had done his prayers and even fasted all that day. He always said that he did not remember even one day in his life when had not performed these obligations during this month.

That very cold night was very different from other nights. It was darker. The blackness of that night was indescribable. My grandfather was completely aware that he would pass away that certain night. It was very late at night, and I was sleeping. But, because of all the noise, I woke up and jumped out of bed. Still after so many years of remembering that night, my heart breaks, and it brings tears to my eyes. My father and my youngest uncle were taking my grandfather to the hospital. My father, who had spoken with my grandfather for hours earlier that night, seemed very distressed and was repeatedly telling others to hurry up.

Suddenly I ran toward my grandfather and started to kiss his hands. I remember that he had tears in his eyes, but I never understood if he was crying from sadness or because of the pain of his sickness. I was already crying and saying, "Don't take him, God." But after a few minutes, they were all gone.

My grandfather died the same night in the hospital. His death was a tragedy and a shock for the whole family.

Life went on, but barely, for the whole family after my grandfather's death. Year after year passed by, but we all felt his empty place in our house, missing him and thinking of him in our hearts.

In Iran when somebody passes away, there are four special ceremonies. The first ceremony is on the third day, the second ceremony on the seventh day, the third one on the fortieth day, and then the anniversary. How grand and special the ceremonies are depends on the economic status of that person's family—rich, middle class, or poor.

My grandfather's ceremonies were all special and magnificent. All his relatives, friends, students, and colleagues attended the ceremonies. Everyone was sorrowful and cried either with their eyes or in their hearts at his funeral. My grandfather was a wise, compassionate, wonderful counselor for everybody around him.

Still after so many years thinking of my grandfather and remembering him—his smile, his eyes and the way he listened to me when I talked—makes me cry in my heart. He was a sweet grandfather for me but also a fundamentalist Muslim writer and a disciplined, fanatic teacher in Feizieh Theology School. Actually most of my father's relatives were somehow involved with religious positions.

My mother loved her family and her children so much that we were always number one for her which was exactly opposite of my father. For him Islam and the law were primary. My father always said that first and foremost he had to satisfy Allah and his prophets.

My mother also came from a strict family. My other grand-father was an army colonel, a serious man who was so tough that everybody around him, even his own family, was scared of him. He had passed away many years before I was born. Since my mother was his oldest child, she had an obligation to do *Namaz* for him. *Namaz* is the ritual of seventeen times of daily prayer which includes two units at dawn, four units in the early after-noon, four units in the late afternoon, four units after sunset, and three units after dark.

According to Islamic law when one of the parents dies, the oldest child does the Islamic prayer and fasting which the parents did not do for any reason, and it is the oldest child who actually tries to compensate for the missed opportunities of prayers by the parents. And they pray that God would accept those prayers and fasting.

My brothers and sisters were all very faithful Muslims who graduated from the University of Teheran and got married after their studies. My father always said that in order to export Islam to the western countries, Muslims must be well educated and know at least one foreign language to be able to preach Islamic law to other nationalities.

One of my sisters got married to a Mullah. He also had stud-ied theology in Feizieh School. He was a very responsible hus-band for my sister, but his religious manners stopped him from becoming more than a priest. His oldest brother was one of the famous judges in the courts of Teheran.

Obeying the *Shariat* was the most important duty and the

only task that I had in my family and in my life. When I was five years old, I could recognize the melody of the Koran in our house. God and Muhammad were the very first words that I learned to write with no mistake. I was taught to say the name of Muhammad even before I learned to say my parents' names. When I still could not pronounce words properly, I was taught to repeat some Arabic words from the Koran by heart.

My parents felt direly responsible to teach us how to obey God, the Islamic law, Muhammad, and the exact way of living in a Islamic society.

According to the *Shariat,* when I was nine years old, I had to start performing the law, especially the *Namaz,* officially. Of *why?* course, the specific age for the boys is twelve but for the girls it is nine.

I had to learn the correct pronunciation of the Arabic words, especially the words that were related to the *Namaz.* Muslims believe that the *Namaz* would be more powerful if the pronunciation of the words is correct.

I remember how much I asked various questions about heaven and the beginning of the world. Once a week I had a private Koran teacher who was a serious lady. She taught me the Koran, verse by verse. She herself was a teacher in Al-Zahra University. Of course, my father could teach me, but he said if he taught me, then I would not feel like a student. But I used to ask him all my questions, and he always corrected me whenever I read Koranic verses. I also asked questions about Islamic law to my brother-in-law whenever I met him. Sometimes I even went to his office to learn more about Islam, and I enjoyed helping him with his office work. My brother-in-law was an expert in Islamic law, so he answered my questions clearly and precisely, and he always made sure that I understood the answer.

I actually do not remember that I had a real childhood like

most other children. The atmosphere of our house was serious, and most of the time discussions on religious and cultural matters were going on in our house.

Besides, I was the youngest child. Everybody was older than me, and I did not have playmates, so there was really no chance to be a child. I had to grow up a lot faster than my peers. I never played childish games or watched cartoons. Even playing with dolls was too immature for me.

What I had actually learned was how to think about God and how to do my *Namaz* properly, and to read Koranic verses with no mistake.

I was fifteen years old when I entered high school. I remember those days clearly. My life was more varied in high school. Making my parents happy and satisfying them was not my only goal any more. Two days a week I had a private female English teacher. It was a lot cheaper to go to an English institute to study English, but my father did not want the children in my family in the public schools and institutes.

If we were outside the house, we should be at school or in the library in the university; and when we went to visit our relatives, either my mother or my father was along with us. We actually had all necessities and facilities in our house, everything that made life comfortable and happy.

All my studies and visiting were under total supervision. I do not recall that I stayed in a friend's house for even one night. If there were an instructive movie going on in the cinema, we were not allowed to go; we had to wait until it came on video and then we could buy it and watch it at home.

I also have lots of memories from the month of *Moharam* which is the first month of the Islamic year. It is a holy month for *Shia* Muslims.

In this month, our house was full of religious activities. Muslims wear black, and they mourn for an Imam's martyrdom. My parents had *Nazr* every year. In the Persian language *Nazr* means "swear to an oath" and it can be done in different ways. Three cooks came to cook the food. Then the food is divided among the poor and neighbors. Many Muslims even believe that eating that food is special for their soul and might even heal the sick.

My brother-in-law, who was a priest, was especially very active during those days. He was always a very big help for my parents during those days. The whole family, my brothers and sisters, stayed in our house overnight during nights of *Moharam*. Muslims believe that even helping in those religious activities would be a great virtue in front of God. *Sadly "Christians" also too often feel the same!*

During the nights of *Moharam* we stayed up very late and we spoke and discussed different matters. I cannot say that I did not enjoy those days and nights, but that joy did not last very long in my life.

In the next chapter you will read why all my joy lasted only until I became seventeen years old.

Another holy month for Muslims is *Ramadan* which is the ninth month of the Islamic year. Muslims believe that Gabriel revealed the Koranic verses to Muhammad in the month of *Ramadan*.

Muslims start to fast from the beginning of this month until the end of the month. They eat only once before the sunrise and once after the sunset. We all fasted in the family during month of *Ramadan*. I loved to fast, but it was so hard for me to wake up in those very early mornings.

Eating before sunrise was another difficult thing to do. But the law in my religion always made me wake up before sunrise to do my *Namaz*. I could hear the voice of the Koran from the radio, repeating the morning prayer. I could also hear the voice of spoon and fork when my family was eating before sunrise in order to get prepared for the fasting day. Those voices are still in my ears. After so many years, when I still remember those days and nights, those sunrises and those sunsets, my heart fills with great sorrow. I become so sorrowful that I kneel down in front of my Lord. I cry, beg and pray to God: "SAVE THOSE MUSLIMS WHO ARE IMPRISONED IN THE DARK WORLD OF ISLAM. LORD, SAVE THEM. ALSO SAVE MY FAMILY."

Very few times when I did not wake up to do my *Namaz* before the sunrise, I had to do the morning–*Namaz* the same time with the noon–*Namaz;* but, of course, there is not so much virtue in the prayer that is not done at the certain time according to law. Muslims are not sure that God would accept that certain *Namaz* because it was not done in the specified time.

Ramadan turns during the different months of the year. If it were in the season of summer, then it was quite difficult to fast in those hot days of summer in Teheran. It was hard not to drink even one drop of water during those long and hot days of summer. Of course, not all Muslims live according to the law and obey the *Shariat,* wake up before the sunrise to perform their prayer and fast during those months of *Ramadan.*

I loved God with all my heart and I truthfully wanted to have a very close relationship with him. The hope of being close to God always encouraged me and made me obey the whole *Shariat.*

Sometimes my youngest brother ate during the day in *Ramadan* when everybody was fasting. That happened only few times but still when he ate, he told everybody that he was fasting.

During the days of *Ramadan,* my mother started cooking in the early afternoon. Although she was fasting herself, she always tried to prepare the most delicious food for the family. She tried hard that everything would be ready for *Eftar,* the end of a fasting day when, according to law, it is permissible to eat. My mother never let my sisters and me help her. She always said that it was enough for us to fast. She knew that performing *Shariat* was difficult. She never asked us to help her with the housework and she felt very responsible for it although she was hungry and thirsty herself during the *Ramadan*. We had a maid to help with the housework, but my father liked my mother to cook. She always said that as long as we obeyed the Islamic law and remained faithful Muslims, she would be very glad and would not feel the tiredness at all.

At *Azan* time, the call to the ritual prayer in the evening, we were allowed to eat the delicious food which my mother had cooked. She was very careful that everything was ready for *Eftar*. My father always read the Koran with a loud voice just before we all started to eat. Sometimes I even saw him crying while reading the Koran. During the month of *Ramadan*, he used to read the whole Koran because at the end of the month he should have finished reading the whole book.

I was happy with what I believed. I actually did not like the kind of life that many young people lived. I tried to live as a perfect symbol of a Muslim girl. I had a loving family who cared about me a lot and I was growing up in a family where I never felt any financial problems. I actually could have anything I wanted and anything I hoped for.

Basically life was perfect. I obeyed the law and the *Shariat* because I loved God with all my heart. I wanted to be as close as possible to him. All I was asking God was for a real connection and relationship. Every single time I wanted to perform my *Namaz*, I closed the door of my room and let the cassette of the Koran be played. I concentrated carefully on the Arabic words to pronounce them correctly. I never thought about anything else but God and his prophet Muhammad during my prayers, but unfortunately it never happened—never. No matter how hard and carefully I prayed and obeyed the Islamic law and the *Shariat* or how hard I concentrated on my Islamic faith, it never happened.

That real relationship with God that I prayed and hoped for during my Islamic faith and life never happened.

CHAINS OF LAW

I cannot believe the blackness of the walls of law that had surrounded my soul and my life. Every time I started to contemplate my religious life and my personal relationship with God, I felt that I had nothing more than a forgotten existence with Him. Although my family provided everything, everything that I wished to have in this world, I always had a feeling that there was something missing in my life.

I was born into and grew up in a wealthy family. Although I always had lavish things in my room, I wore the finest clothes at all times, and my family was loving and caring, I always felt and knew that there was something missing in that type of life.

I never believed the blackness of my religious life would continue, and I always hoped for a door that would open to a world where I was not a forgotten being anymore.

I studied Islamic law and the Koran for many years but besides all that, I decided to start doing systematic studies in different ideologies.

All I was asking and looking for was a two-way relationship with God, a relationship where I could speak with mighty God in my mother language.

I remember the day that I stood up and asked God, "WHY DO

I HAVE TO SPEAK TO YOU AND PRAY IN ARABIC?" That day was
the beginning of a revolution in my Islamic faith.

On one of the coldest days in winter when I came home from
school, I prepared myself as usual to do my *Namaz*. I had to perform my ablutions before the prayer. The ablution is called
Vouzoo in Persian which includes washing the face and then the
arms to the elbows, rubbing the wet hands through the hair, and
washing the feet.

In fanatic Muslim families, every member of the family has a
personal prayer carpet and women have their personal veils. They
usually do not use each other's veils. I also had my own veil,
prayer carpet, and expensive Koran that I had gotten as a birthday present from my father.

I remember that very cold day clearly. It is as though it were
yesterday when I switched on the tape recorder to hear some verses from the Koran in order to be able to concentrate to start my
Namaz. I was going to do the eight noon and evening prayers. I
performed four which belonged to noon *Namaz*, and I was in the
middle of my evening *Namaz* when I felt a very deep heaviness
on my heart. I felt something that I cannot explain with words.
Clouds of deep sorrow blanketed my heart. I had become so sad
and disappointed that I suddenly sat down on the floor on my
prayer carpet and started to cry.

I have never forgotten how loud I was crying. I was so full of
fear and doubt that I stopped my prayer and so sorrowful that I
asked God, "WHY DO I HAVE TO SPEAK TO YOU IN ARABIC?
DO YOU ONLY UNDERSTAND THE ARABIC LANGUAGE? DOES-
N'T THE KORAN SAY THAT YOU ARE THAT MIGHTY ONE WHO
UNDERSTANDS EVERYTHING?" As I was crying and repeating
the name of Allah, I hit my fist on the floor and asked Allah one
more time, "WHY DO I HAVE TO USE ARABIC AS A CREDIT, AND
WHY DO I HAVE TO BE AN ARAB UNTIL YOU ACCEPT ME?"

That day I was too sad to continue my prayers. The law says if a Muslim stops and breaks off the *Namaz* for any reason except a matter of life and death, one has to start the whole prayer all over again. I had broken off the *Namaz* in the middle, but I had chosen to tell my grievances and ask the Mighty One to show me a small sign, a simple answer to all those prayers that I had tried at all times to so determinedly concentrate on. I looked for a tiny sign that I never saw and a simple answer that I never got. I had the feeling that all my hopes were nothing but empty dreams.

An inner revolution had started inside me. I did not want to be a cautious Muslim and a conservative person who spent her whole life in fear and compulsory silence. I knew that I was born to a free existence, not a life as a sewn lip prisoner who never questions the Koran and Muhammad and is imprisoned in the chains of law and rules.

All I was asking for was some results for all those prayers that I had carefully done since my childhood, some results in reality. I had to find out more about God and his prophet's life. I had become turbulent and filled with doubt.

THERE WAS NO FORWARD PROGRESS BUT NO LASTING PEACE IN REMAINING WHERE I WAS.

I had already broken off my *Namaz* for the first time. The heaviness that had started in my heart brought so much doubt inside me. I actually could not understand what that heaviness was or how it started. I just knew that it had made me so sad and angry.

I did not finish my prayer that day. I put my prayer carpet aside and took out the newspaper to read. I did not want to think about what had happened to me or what had happened to my prayer that afternoon. I felt so worried and sad for not doing my prayer; it was the first time that I had not done it. I hoped that my curiosity would pass so that I could perform the law and rules with no question just like my brothers and sisters and thousands of other Muslims.

Performing *Namaz* and all the other prayers was supposed to give me a feeling of reverence, a feeling of assurance about who I was and where I was going, an assurance that I was on the straight path to paradise and a real relationship with God. But unfortunately, I found all those feelings and realities just empty words, empty dreams that never came true.

It was obvious that in my Islamic faith I always had the opportunity to speak with God, but the most difficult part was that Allah never answered me or my questions.

The same exact day that I felt that heaviness in my heart, my sister and her husband were supposed to come to our house for dinner. After dinner I went to my brother-in-law and asked him, "Do you really believe that the Muslims are forgiven and blessed by God through their good deeds?"

Suddenly he looked at me very surprised and after a few seconds he started to laugh and said: "OF COURSE NOT. NONE OF US KNOW IF WE ARE REALLY BLESSED OR NOT. IT IS WRITTEN THAT WE MUST PERFORM THE *SHARIAT* AND BE OBEDIENT TO ALLAH, THAT HE MIGHT HAVE MERCY ON US. BESIDES, WE ARE NOT SUPPOSED TO QUESTION ALLAH AND THE LAW."

I was really sick at heart that my spiritual life was in so much conflict. Not performing the *Namaz* had made me confused and upset. Accomplishing the *Shariat* was actually part of my being and my life. I wanted to be obedient, but I had questions about Islam, and I could not just wink at everything.

I decided to start performing my *Namaz* again in spite of all my doubts, but this time in my mother language, Persian. I had never heard that anyone had done that before, but I did not care if anyone had done it before or not. I did not care what people, even my own family, would think of me if they saw me doing the

Namaz in Persian. But I just remember that everybody who saw me doing *Namaz* in Persian laughed at me. The way that I did my prayer had become a joke for others until my father, who always felt very responsible about his children's private lives, told me that he wanted to speak to me.

One day he angrily came into my room, shut the door and said, "Your behavior is ridiculous. Why are you trying to be so adventurous? ALLAH WILL NEVER ACCEPT YOUR NAMAZ IN PERSIAN. You are making a joke out of a very serious issue such as *Namaz*." I asked my father, "Wouldn't Allah accept such prayer just because it is not done in Arabic? WHY SHOULD I PRAY IN A FOREIGN LANGUAGE THAT I DO NOT EVEN UNDERSTAND THE WORDS? ALLAH IS RACISM HIMSELF THAT ONLY ACCEPTS THE PRAYERS IN ARABIC. IF WE ALL HAVE TO WORSHIP HIM IN ARABIC, THEN HE IS NOT THAT MIGHTY GOD THAT I HAVE LEARNED TO CALL HIM FROM MY CHILDHOOD."

My father, whose face was completely red, stared at me angrily and said, "Don't ever discuss about the way of performing *Namaz* or even the other rules in Islam again, and never question God again. This is the end of discussion." He went out of the room and shut the door. Still sitting on the chair in my room, I was choked with tears. *One hurts with him, however...*

Almost all the Muslims memorize the Arabic words without even understanding the meanings of *Namaz* or Koran and only the ones who have studied Arabic as a foreign language can understand the meanings. My father was a translator and he had studied Arabic for years, but how many Muslims have studied Arabic as a foreign language? Most Muslims just repeat the Arabic words that they have memorized, and they perform their *Namaz* without even knowing the meanings.

Arabic itself is as important as *Shariat* because if someone wants to worship Allah through reading Koran, it must be read in *control!*

Arabic. Otherwise, to get information and learn about different chapters and verses, it can be read in other languages or different translations. But to worship Allah, the Koran must be read in Arabic and no other language.

My Koran teacher came to our house once a week. She interpreted every single verse systematically. Once a week for two hours I studied the Koran privately with my teacher, but all those religious lessons and all those Koranic interpretations not only did not obliterate the dark points from my mind, they also made me realize how far Allah was from me.

I always thought that slavery was only allocated to the eighteenth century, but I actually considered myself a slave in the world of Islam, especially because I was a female. I was one of those thousands of slaves who was disappointedly looking and hoping for a way that could fulfill the desire for freedom with which I was created.

Muslims try to be better than each other. There is always a competition going on in their hearts and in their daily lives. This competition covers society, culture, and all different aspects of life.

In Islam Allah's blessing is supposed to be gained through good deeds. Muslims strenuously try to please Allah, and even themselves, through performing religious duties.

In the world of Islam, freedom belongs mostly to men. Women are not counted in society. My brothers were not so much under control as I was, not by my parents and not by society. The darkness of religion is not that heavy for men. They are the ones who are respected and counted; perhaps that is the reason that Muslim men are not sensitive to most of the problems in Islamic societies.

I never did my religious duties to be seen and appreciated by others. I did the law because I loved Allah. I was sure that he was somewhere, but I could not, or had not, found him yet.

Days and nights passed by, as did winter and spring. Trees budded and sprouts came up. Trees which had become barren in wintertime all at once became splendid and full of leaves in spring, and I who had grasped that religion was totally and absolutely nonsense was still looking and hoping for a way to be released.

I was wondering if there was a way of deliverance. In that journey, different philosophic opinions drew my attention since religion had become an empty path to me.

One day a friend invited me to go to her house for lunch. They had a big library with many books. I knew that she had communistic ideas, but I did not know that she was serious about them. We discussed communism in detail, and I remember that I was so disturbed that I even did not desire to continue the discussion with her.

I had never doubted God's existence, not even for one moment in my life. Although I did not know how to reach him, I was completely sure that it was I who was at fault for not reaching him yet.

In my Koran class, my teacher had almost finished the interpretation of the whole Koran. We had only a few *Suras*, chapters of the Koran, left to finish the book, and I still had not found a solution for my doubts and questions.

Nature was the most beautiful creation of God for me. I could sit beside the river for hours and listen to the birds singing and the leaves of the trees when the wind was blowing. I loved all of God's creation. The sound of rain falling could steal all my thoughts and capture my heart. For some time I thought that I might find that hidden God in nature or at least in literature.

In that period of life, poetry had become a safe shelter for me.

Poets showed me in the most beautiful and brave way that life is filled with hurts. Humanity is of little value because of the lack of intellect. The most ingenious philosophers have explored and sought answers to the sorrows of life, but NOBODY HAS HAD THE BRAVERY YET TO OFFER HIS THOUGHTS ON HOW WE CAN SOLVE THESE. FINALLY, WHAT IS THE WAY FOR OUR SORROWS TO BE OVERCOME?

I never wanted to be a religious person who could not be sure of being blessed by God or not. It was my hope and desire to recognize the power of Almighty God and especially find out how I could reach him.

Intense loneliness had come to me. I used to do most of my reading and studying at night. I was accustomed to night. In that loneliness and darkness that I surrounded me, I had opened the gates of my thoughts to philosophy, gnosticism, and any sort of thoughts that you can imagine.

I read the poems of Omar Khayam, one of the most wonderful poets in the world, who says:

A MUEZZIN FROM THE TOWER OF DARKNESS CRIES,

"FOOLS! YOUR REWARD IS NEITHER HERE NOR THERE!"

So what was the way then? I was wondering why we had come into this world and where we should seek refuge in it.

All my dreams were imprinted on the sandy strand where one wave could change everything. In the solitude of those days, I looked for a roaring river that could wash away the field of my thoughts.

I HAD LEARNED THAT GOING IS THE CONTINUATION OF BEING . . . BUT GOING TO WHERE, GOING TO WHOM?!

I was truly wondering where the valley of knowledge and assurance lay.

AN EVERLASTING SUNSET

The library was my second house. It was the only place where I could stay as long as I wanted to. One afternoon when I came home from school, we had *Rozeh* in our house. *Rozeh* is a meeting for the commemoration of the martyrs of *Karbela* in which a professional narrator describes and explains in a very special way all the details of the tragedies which were related to Imams in Karbela.

My parents had invited some people to come to the meeting. Every month, on the first Thursday of the month, we had a *Rozeh* to which about forty or fifty people came. Women and men were in separate rooms.

The priest who was invited to explain about those tragedies every month in our house was Ayatolla Nategh-Noori, who was the chief of the parliament in Iran at the moment. My brother-in-law always attended those meetings with some of his colleagues.

Those activities did not make me happy like they did in the old days. I had understood that no matter how hard and how fast I tried to run to reach God through the law and my good deeds, the more distance that came into existence between God and me.

We had to be present in the house when there was *Rozeh;* otherwise, we had to have a very good reason for not being there. The day of that meeting meant a lot to my parents.

That day I did not want to be present in that meeting, so I told my mother that I had to go to the library. My mother insisted that I stay and listen to the *Rozeh*. But I told her that I had to go to the library to prepare myself for the exam that I was going to have in a few days.

Contrary to my mother's request, I went to the library. She told me that she would be worried until I came back home. I never understood what she was so worried about on that day.

In the library something very unexpected happened. As I was sitting and preparing my studies, by accident I noticed that there was a book on the floor under the table. Of course, I do not call it an accident now, but a miracle. As I bent to get that book, I thought surely it belonged to someone who had dropped it and had forgotten to take it. There was no mark of the library on the book. I looked at the cover to see what kind of book it was. The name of the book seemed very strange to me.

On the cover of the book was written *INJIL SHARIF* which is Holy Bible in the Persian language. It was the first time that I had seen such a book. It was not familiar to me at all. I turned over the first page, but I did not understand anything. I had seen the Bible in French and English before, but I had never seen it in Persian before. I still was not exactly what the book was about.

I was amazed, and I went to the lady who was in charge in the library. I showed her the book and asked if it belonged to the library or someone who had forgotten to take it. I even insisted on giving it to her to put with the missing books if it did not belong to the library, but she said that they did not keep missing books. She insisted that I could take it home and read it. I loved reading so I took the book home very happily. I thought that it would be very interesting to read that book.

When I came home the *Rozeh* was finished, and all the people were gone. My parents were very tired. My mother had cried so much that her eyes were swollen. It always broke my heart when I saw my mother's tears fall down her cheeks in a *Rozeh* or during the *Namaz*. She always said that she felt her prayers would be granted when she cried. When she started crying, she had no control over her tears. I always hoped that there was a way that I could stop those tears.

My brother-in-law and my sister were still in our house. They were all sitting in the livingroom with my parents. I joined them and suddenly I remembered the book that I had found. I myself was so surprised that there was a Bible in Persian that I thought I would show it to others too.

As soon as I took the book out of my bag, before saying even one word, I saw my father's face turned red like fire. My-brother-in law took the book from me and said, "A Bible in Persian!"

Immediately I said that I never knew that there was a Bible in Persian. My father asked where I had gotten it, and I explained what had happened in the library. My father said, "We respect this book, but it is not ours. It is not our holy book." Immediately he said that I should take it back where I had gotten it from, and he added that he never wanted to see that book again in our house.

I was wondering why everyone was so hard on that book. My younger brother said, "What is wrong if somebody wants to read the book just to get some more information?" Suddenly my father who was already very angry said with a very loud voice, "I will never let my daughter read the Bible. There is enough information in Koran. We do not need the other's holy book to get more information."

Then I understood what a bad idea it was to show the book in the first place. I was angry with myself for showing the book. I could have just hidden the book and read it later. But the reaction of my family had made me even more curious to read the book and find out what it was about.

I took the book back from my brother-in-law who was still holding and looking at it. My father wanted to keep the book. He said that we were not allowed to have that book at home. But I asked him to let me to take the book back to the library since I had found it there.

Although my father was so angry and sad, I do not know what happened inside him. In that moment, he gave me the book back and said I must take it back tomorrow, and he never ever wanted to see such a book again in my hand. My brother-in-law added that I should learn how to stay immune against different subjects that could affect my Islamic beliefs.

I had the whole night to find out what was written in that book and what had made everyone so disturbed and angry. The reaction of my parents had made me even more curious to read that book. If they had not behaved like that, I probably would have not bothered to read the book. I believe that God wanted me to show the book that night, so by their reaction I was compelled to start reading it right away.

That night I waited until the last light went out. I went to the kitchen after a flashlight. I had firmly decided to read the book but no one could find out about it; otherwise, I was in big trouble. I could not turn on the light because then my parents would have understood that I was still awake and they would know that I was reading the Bible. I had to wait until everyone went to sleep before I could start reading.

I could not really understand why everyone was so sensitive about the book that I had found. I had many different books in my library, but no one in the family had been disturbed by them. When I was studying other religious philosophies, my parents had seen those books in my hand, but they never warned me not to read those books, even when they saw me reading about communism. Perhaps knowing how much I loved God with all my heart was a relief for them.

I remember that night so clearly when I had determined to read the book that I had found. At the last minute before my mother went to go to her room to sleep, she insisted that I not forget to take the book back in the morning before any problem started in the family.

I always felt very comfortable with my mother. She truly had a difficult responsibility at home. Keeping everybody happy and satisfied was not an easy job to do. I always felt pity for her. That night I asked my mother if she wanted to read that book. She replied that since Islam is the last and most perfect religion, she did not even want to read the book. And she added that there were verses in the Bible that could confuse my Islamic beliefs. I never understood how she knew about those verses if she had not read the Bible before. I never got the chance to ask her about that.

That night as soon as everybody went to sleep, I opened the book and started to read by flashlight. The first chapter was a genealogy. I skipped reading that, and I started from the birth of Jesus Christ. I was planning to finish the whole book by morning since I still had not decided if I wanted to keep the Bible or not. But after a few hours reading, I got really tired and I had lots of pain in my hands since I had to hold the flashlight in one hand and the Bible in the other hand in order to read it.

I remember I read so much that I fell asleep. When I opened my eyes, it was seven o'clock in the morning. The book had fallen down on the floor, and I was so tired that I could not move my body.

As soon as I fixed my eyes on the Bible on the floor, I heard my mother calling me from downstairs. I remembered that I had to take the book back, and I was confused about what to do. While I was getting ready for the school, I decided to keep the

Bible and finish what I had started to read, but I had to find a good place to hide the Bible.

I can never do anything right if I am in a hurry. One more time I heard my mother calling me. I was both angry and hasty. I thought the safest place would be under the mattress.

While I was having my breakfast, my mother reminded me one more time not to forget to take the book back. After I left home, I was very worried about the Bible that I had hidden. I did not often close the door of my room, and my mother would come and go into my room a few times a day.

What would happen if they found out about the book that I had hidden? The question was on my mind all day long, and it disturbed me very much.

I was not even sure if it was worth it to go through all that trouble just to read the book. But there was some power which was making me read the Bible.

A power made me do that. As soon as my hours in school were finished, I rushed home. My mother saw me, and the very first thing that she asked was if I had taken the book back. She seemed very pleased and happy when she heard that the book was taken back. I had never lied to her before; that was the first time. I was very upset about that because she was the most wonderful mother, and I did not want to lie to her.

I remember that during those days, I used every minute of my life to read the Bible. That day in the afternoon I went to my room and read the book of Luke. Before my father came home from work, I had the best opportunity to read. There was not much opportunity to read that book since most of the time we had guests in our house, and if we did not have any guests, my brothers and sisters were always there with their families.

As I read through the Bible, I was fascinated by Jesus himself and especially his character, his justice, and his way of life. I was fascinated because he was not born out of lust. He never got married, never fought, and did not kill anyone. He never owned anything and was not greedy for power. I was fascinated by his love and his forgiveness. All those miracles of restoring the blind and bringing the dead to life meant a lot to me. And most important of all, I was reading the Bible in Persian, my own mother language.

Because I was a Muslim, I had to read Koran in Arabic if I wanted to read it in order to worship Allah, and not only I, but all Muslims have to do the same if they want to worship Allah. So, I was wondering in which language the Christians read the Bible when they intend to worship God.

Although I had problems and questions about my Islamic faith and I was truly fascinated by Jesus Christ, I was fighting hard with myself not to be naive.

I was trying hard to be a perfect Muslim, a perfect Muslim who always kept the law and was obedient to the *Shariat*. I always tried hard not to break anybody's heart. I loved justice, and I had tried all my life to be a good person.

While I was reading the Bible, although huge question marks came in to my mind, I still continued carrying out all the Islamic rules. But this time I obeyed, not with all my heart, but because from my childhood Islamic society and my parents had whispered in my ears that I had to perform my Islamic duties no matter what.

I still stood towards Mecca and performed my *Namaz* and repeated the worshipping words of *Namaz*, not in Arabic, but in my own mother language. Meanwhile my parents thought that I had stopped doing the *Namaz* in Persian.

Reading the Bible had taken all my concentration, and very soon I finished reading it. I was very happy that finally, with all those difficulties, I made it. I finished reading that wonderful book because of the miracle which had happened in my favorite place, the library, where I had found the book.

I used every moment of my life to read the Bible, late at night and even in the bathroom. I remember that I never got enough sleep during that period of my life when I was reading the Bible. I was tired all the time.

It was my last year in the school and I had only two months left to graduate. I was studying hard for the final exams.

While I was reading the Bible at that time, I thought there must be some Christians living in Iran. I knew enough about the Armenians, but I could not accept them as true followers of Jesus Christ since I knew that they were only a nation who had inherited religion, just like Muslims. I thought that there must be some Persian-speaking Christians; otherwise, the Bible in Persian would not exist. I was excited about meeting at least one person who was truly following Jesus Christ.

The cold days of winter were almost gone and the spring with all its beauties was coming. The birds were coming back from their winter quarters, and the weather was getting warm. The wonderful smell of spring was spread everywhere.

During those days I was also preparing for marriage. In fundamentalist families children usually get married a young age. Later in life I understood that even my marriage was by God's will. God prepared everything so fast, and I got married within a few days to one who has lived by God's call and has always been a wonderful husband and strong supporter in the ups and downs of life. Since my marriage I have constantly praised God for my dear husband who loves God with all his heart and has stood by me in every moment of life.

In Iran every year the beautiful spring also brings the new year with it. The new year in Iran is called *Narooz* which means

New Day. It is a wonderful time for all the families.

Families get together and have a very special dinner together. My mother used to start cooking early in the morning. Everything for the dinner had to be fresh. On that special night almost all the Iranian families eat *Sabzi Polo*, which is special mixed rice with special vegetables and fresh salmon on the side. Drops of fresh lemon juice give it a wonderful taste. My mother had so much joy while cooking on that day. She always loved to see the whole family together. We stayed long together on that special night, and we all truly had a great time.

The day after, which is the first day of the new year, the younger children go and visit their older relatives, parents and the grandparents. All relatives visit each other, especially those who have not seen each other during the year.

My father used to place new bank notes inside his Koran the night before, and on the first day of the year he gave one bank note and one gift that he had already prepared to each one of his sons and his daughters and sons-in-law and all his nephews.

In Iran they believe that giving money in the new year, especially if it has already been placed inside a Koran, would bring good luck to the one who receives the money.

I had a wonderful time during *Narooz*. The sun shone through that big window which was always my favorite one from my childhood. In those rays of sunshine I used to rest on the big, comfortable couch in the livingroom. The coffee table in the middle of the room was decorated with the best and most delicious kinds of pastries, dried nuts, fruits of spring and the most savory chocolates which were bought from the best confectionery in town.

The best hours of my rest were in that livingroom. I have not yet forgotten the wonderful smell of the big bunch of flowers which was placed in the middle of the table and the beautiful, kind face of my mother who liked to organize the livingroom in the afternoon when everybody else was resting.

My mother made sure that the house was clean and organized, especially during the days of the New Year. She was very hospitable and she loved *Narooz* because of all the guests who came. Every guest who came to our house had a bunch of flowers in hand, and the guests brought great joy with them into my parent's heart. Buying flowers is an important part of Iranian custom. The flower shops and confectioners do their best business during the days of *Narooz*.

How much I miss those days when I think about it! It seems like all those memories were just yesterday. The warmth of the sunshine from my favorite window in that livingroom, the smell of those beautiful flowers and the happiest smile on my parents' faces will never be forgotten in my mind.

I was planning to continue my studies in the university, but life does not always go on as we plan.

I had read the Bible once. Of course, I did not understand everything, but I was thirsty to know more. Unfortunately I could not share what I had read with anyone, but I considered carefully whatever I read.

In spite of the fact that I had finished the Bible once, there were some chapters that I was interested in reviewing. But I was tired just reading it, especially parts which I did not understand.

In Matthew 11: 28 when I read that Jesus Christ said, "COME TO ME ALL YOU WHO ARE WEARY AND BURDENED, AND I WILL GIVE YOU REST," I wondered what the writer meant by "burdened." Did he mean the ones who were burning in the fire of recognition like me or some other people with other kinds of pains?

I was eager to know more and meet someone with whom I could share about what I had read.

During one of the warmest days in the spring, it was noon and time for *Namaz*. I went to my room and knelt down before God. I started to pray and entreat God. I will never forget that prayer. I will always remember it, word by word:

"GOD, I AM NOT TRULY SURE WHETHER YOU ARE HEARING ME OR NOT. I HAVE NEVER SUCCEEDED IN KNOWING YOU. I DON'T KNOW IF I AM FEARFUL BEFORE YOU OR NOT. RIGHT NOW WHILE I AM PRAYING, I AM NOT SURE THAT I EVEN KNOW MYSELF ANYMORE. I HAVE ALWAYS BEEN IMPRISONED IN A PRISON OF WHICH RELIGION AND LAW ARE THE JAILERS. MY FEET ARE TIRED OF TAKING MORE STEPS. TAKE MY HANDS TO REACH YOU. I DO NOT KNOW ANY MORE WHERE I CAN FIND YOU, BUT YOU KNOW WHERE I AM."

And I prayed that prayer with all I had from the bottom of my heart.

The same day my mother said that she had invited my sister with her husband and also my brother-in-law's family to our house. They were three brothers, two of whom were priests, and the oldest brother was a judge in the courts of Teheran. They had only one sister who was studying medicine in the University of Teheran, and it was her last year before she graduated. The whole family was fundamentalist Muslim and very wealthy.

After the lunch we were all sitting in the livingroom and were drinking tea. My brother-in-law's sister was named Monir. We had a very close relationship, but of course it was limited also. Monir was graduating from the university very soon and had lots of academic experience. She always advised me about how to prepare for final exams and get ready for entering the university. She explained to me the proper way of studying.

Until that day, we had never told each other what was going on in the bottom of our hearts. I remember that while we were all sitting in the livingroom and talking, Monir said that finally, after so many years, she had gotten her hair cut. She always had long hair, so I was very surprised and wanted to see her hair. Since she was wearing a veil, we had to go to my room so that she could take her veil off.

As soon as she entered my room, I noticed the Bible which was still on the table. I had forgotten to hide it after reading it the last time. Although I was so careful, for the first time I had forgotten to hide it. Monir had already seen the book before I could do anything.

My brother-in-law had told his family how I had found a Bible in the library. Monir went toward the table and took the book. I begged her with my eyes not to tell anyone about it. But for a fanatic girl like Monir, from a fundamentalist family, my entreaty would not mean anything.

She had the Bible in her hands, and I was afraid what my father was going to do after all those lies that I had told them. For a moment I truly preferred to die and not to see my mother's face. She had trusted me the whole time. Monir and I were best friends, but when it is a matter of religion among fundamentalist families, friendship means nothing. That lovely afternoon had turned into a dark hell for me.

Monir looked at the Bible with a face full of questions and surprises. I was not sure what she was going to do. While she seemed shaken, she took a few steps and sat on my bed.

She had a very strange look on her face, and her eyes were almost wet with tears. She took her eyes off of the Bible for a short moment and asked me, "Do you read this book?" I did not know what to answer. I had really never learned to lie about anything in my life before, but for the sake of reading the Bible, I had already lied to my mother once. But that day a very strange power inside me made me tell Monir the truth. I did not know why I trusted her.

I told her how I had found the Bible in the library and what had happened the night that I brought it home. I also told her that something made me keep the book and read it. I explained how I had read it with a flashlight during night time.

She was completely quiet when I told her that reading the Bible made me think about God and His creation in a different way. I added that nobody in the family knew that I had kept the Bible and had read it.

Suddenly I saw the sweetest smile on her face; she was smiling so broadly that I will never forget that smile. I had actually never seen her face so trustworthy before. I understood that there had to be something that she had not told me about her life.

While she was turning over the pages of the Bible, she looked at me and said, "Let me tell you a secret. I have been following Jesus Christ for eight years, but my faith has always been a secret."

I was shocked by what Monir had said. I looked at her veil one more time and then looked at Monir again and asked her, "Are you saying that you are a Christian?" While I was both surprised and happy, I said, "But how?" Her face, shining from happiness, looked at me deeply and said, "Through the miracles of the Lord, my sister."

She said that she had Christian friends, and they met once a week. She also told me very briefly how she had become a Christian through a pastor who led the church in Meshhad, which is a holy city in Iran. She also told me how she had found out about Muslims who converted to Christianity and explained how God had changed her whole life.

Monir, who was twenty-eight years old, was studying medicine and soon she was going to graduate from the university and she was going to become a doctor. She was very smart girl who was converted in the name of Jesus Christ but was still wearing a veil, especially in front of her fundamentalist family. She said that she had to pretend that she did the law; otherwise, she would be rejected by her family and the university and would be killed because of her faith.

She said at the time that she accepted Christ in her heart, God gave her the wisdom to continue wearing the veil. She was actually an evangelist; however, since she was very active in her faith and all her prayers were done in the name of Jesus Christ. Then I understood why she was so shocked when she saw the Bible in my room and I understood why I had trusted her to tell the truth.

MONIR WAS A CONVERTED MUSLIM WHO WAS STILL WEARING THE VEIL BUT PRAYED IN THE NAME OF JESUS CHRIST AND STOOD FOR HER FAITH UNTIL THE LAST MOMENT OF HER LIFE.

As soon as we heard that somebody was coming upstairs, Monir hid the Bible under the mattress. I was surprised because she hid it the same place that I always hid that Bible. Monir and I truly had a lot in common after that day.

We were both born in fundamentalist Muslim families and we had lots of similarities in our lives. Then we could share a lot about the Christian faith.

That day after our conversation, when we wanted to go downstairs to join the rest of the family, Monir took my hands and said: "Jesus will show himself to you sooner or later. Do you know why? Because he is alive. HALLELUJAH!" I heard that word for the first time from Monir.

That day I really did not understand what Monir meant by saying those things, but I was very amazed by what had happened. For eight years Monir was following Jesus in such a fundamentalist family. How could that really be possible while having two priest brothers? I wondered how difficult it had been for her to follow Christ. I was truly grateful to God for Monir. At least

I could share all my thoughts with her and ask all my questions. Then I understood that there must be other people also like Monir who were following Christ in their hearts but they still wore their veil.

My intellectual acquaintance with Monir entailed a lot of joy for me, but there was actually a painful end which is unforgettable in my whole life and it will be on my heart forever.

One day after their visit in our house, I promised Monir that I would call her. She invited me to go to their meeting on Thursday evening. It was very exciting for me to attend a Christian fellowship since I was very tired of trying and running after God by myself.

The meeting started at six o'clock. I could not tell my parents where I was planing to go. I met Monir at five o'clock and we had to take the bus to the north part of town. There were about nine people in a small apartment. Three of them were men and the rest were women.

As soon as we got there, Monir took her veil off. It was hard for me to believe, although I knew that she was not a Muslim anymore. I was wearing a veil too, but I sat down the way I was and I did not take it off. Actually I was so accustomed to wearing the veil that it had become part of my being and I never thought I could take it off.

Monir introduced me to others and they all welcomed me very warmly. A middle-aged man, whom everybody called Ali, started the meeting. Although it was the first time that I met them, I had a feeling that I knew them already. Their warmth was very interesting to me. They began to sing some very happy songs. They were beautiful songs. I loved to hear more and I liked the words of the songs very much. While I was amazed with the way of their singing, Ali turned to me and gave me a thicker Bible than I had found in the library and asked me to read a verse from book of Psalms:

"SERVE THE LORD WITH GLADNESS; COME BEFORE HIM WITH JOYFUL SONGS." Psalm 100:2

I was sure that Monir had explained about me before we went there and probably Ali had felt how surprised I was by their songs in that meeting.

Then Ali spoke about salvation and the price that Jesus Christ paid for our sins. For the very first time, I heard that we were all sinners. The meeting was kind of strange for me, but it was not far from what I had been thinking. Of course, Monir had spoken to me about some biblical issues before we went to that meeting.

At the end of the meeting, I asked Ali what he meant by saying that we were all sinners. He explained very simply but in the most perfect way. I just could not believe how friendly and warmly they had accepted me among themselves even though I was wearing the veil and my appearance was very different from theirs. They truly showed how glad they were that I was there.

On the way home we spoke a lot about the meeting. In that period of life, Monir and I spent a lot of time together. I was very happy that I finally had found a wonderful friend like Monir with whom I could share what I was reading in the Bible. I was also glad for finding some other Christians and especially Ali who could answer all my questions so clearly.

The day after the meeting Ali gave me his number and two books about Christian faith which again I had to hide at home and read them in hiding. For a few months I attended their meetings, their prayers and their Bible studies.

One day Monir said that they would have a guest from Meshhad who was pastoring the church in that city, one of the most holy cities in northeast of Iran. His name was Pastor Hossein Soodmand. For me it was the first time to meet a Christian pastor. I had seen my grandfather and my brother-in-law and some other relatives who were priests, but to meet a Christian pastor who was a Muslim before was very surprising for me. I was actually very excited to meet him.

That evening when we went to that meeting, I met a person whose humility and understanding stole all my heart at the first moment. Before he said anything, his face and his silence were preaching the love of God. He was so nice and kind that I felt I had known him for some years and felt that I could trust him more than anybody else. He was Pastor Soodmand that Monir was speaking about and had come to the Lord through. He had a wonderful smile on his face when he spoke about the Bible and tears in his eyes when he heard how I had found that Bible in the library. Then he heard what I had gone through just to read the Bible and heard more about my background. With his humble eyes, kind smile and warm words, he encouraged me a lot as he explained briefly what he himself had gone through for his Christian faith.

That evening Pastor Soodmand spoke a lot with me and told me that God had chosen me and said that everything which had happened was part of God's plan from the day that I had found the Bible in that library. That evening Pastor Soodmand prayed with me and I gave my heart to Christ. I still had questions and I had not understood some verses in the Bible but something strange, a wonderful feeling inside me, drew me to that prayer.

For the first time I prayed in that group. Pastor Soodmand put his hand on me and prayed for me, a prayer so strong that my whole body was shaking after that prayer.

Monir had come to Christ through Pastor Soodmand and she was very much in contact with him and received Christian materials from him. Pastor Soodmand meant a lot to her and the whole group and even to me although I had been in that group for only a few months. He always struggled for others' success and said that his happiness is to serve others rather than to be served.

He took every step of his life in order to glorify God and bring more fruit for the name of Christ.

Pastor Soodmand gave his number to me and I started to call to Meshhad and speak to him on the phone. He always gave wonderful teachings and advice on the phone. I remember the last time that I met him, he said, "Every Muslim who comes to Christ is a miracle. Jesus has released you from all the laws and rules and never let anybody or anything take away the freedom that Jesus has given you."

Pastor Hossein Soodmand was fifty-five years old and was martyred on the third of December 1990, charged with apostasy by the fundamentalists. For four weeks he was subjected to torture and abuse. Then he was released on bail but again arrested and imprisoned and finally executed by hanging after a month. Even his wife Mahtab, who is blind, and his four children were not informed until after the execution took place. Every single time that I have remembered his voice, his look and his strong prayers I can never resist crying.

Many times I have cried and asked God why that happened. But I have decided not to forget his teachings and what he said about the freedom that Jesus has given me. I find comfort whenever I remember that he is with Christ in heaven; to remember that is truly the best relief for me.

At this point I must say that I am proud that I gave my heart to Christ through a man who stood for his faith until the last moment of his life. He stood bravely for his faith and he screamed "JESUS IS ALIVE" until the last moment. He was not timid and he did not run away from this world and its persecutions—just like the other martyrs who stood up for their faith in Iran and were not afraid of claiming what Jesus had done in their lives.

In our meetings we usually had long discussions after the meeting and Ali always tried to explain everything very carefully to me. I always paid attention to how everybody prayed in those meetings. The way that they all prayed was so pure. They all seemed pure and very sure about the way that they had chosen.

I had completely given up my Islamic faith. For many years I thought that I was very good person. I was proud of being a Muslim, tried the best to concentrate on my prayers and be completely obedient to the law. I struggled so much to reach God through my good deeds, but no matter how hard I had practiced my Islamic faith, there was still a deep long distance between God and me. I understood that being born in a fundamentalist family and doing *Namaz* from nine years old and doing it seventeen times a day did not save me and did not take away that distance which was built between God and me.

A strange feeling had started to grow inside me—a feeling between faith and doubt. All those feelings and thoughts happened in the last period of my Islamic faith. I had started to wonder what if I was wrong. I want to explain at this point that, although I had given up my Islamic faith, there were so many questions in my mind about the Islamic area. I tried hard to understand what I was doing. I did not intend to lose all those years that I had obeyed Allah, all those teachings that I had received through my father and grandfather and my teachers.

The day before I gave my life completely to Christ in that evening meeting with Pastor Soodmand, I was really afraid of being so doubtful about the law and the character of Allah in Islam. For some time I thought that standing before God with all those questions was easier than denying my whole faith, but the love among Christians and the Bible's teachings and Pastor Soodmand's advice were so wonderful and unique they that drew me more and more every day.

The love and fellowship of Christians made me think that Jesus' love must be so wonderful and great that his followers have learned to love one another in that special way. I just knew that

I was not proud of my Islamic faith anymore.

When had I really tasted joy and divine peace in my heart when I was a Muslim? . . . I who had done all my prayers and had obeyed the law, had fasted during *Ramadan,* and had performed seventeen times prayer *Namaz* every day since I was nine years old.

I had only one exam left in the school. I had very good grades because I was planning to continue my studies in the university. After my last exam Monir said there would be a celebration on the occasion of a baptismal service in Ali's house. Pastor Hossein Soodmand was also going to be there, and I was one of those who were going to be baptized that day.

Monir came to our house in the evening to stay overnight so we could go there together the day after. That evening Monir and I were sitting in the room of the house where I was born. All my childhood had been spent in that house. It was a house full of great memories. In that beautiful evening while we were sitting in my room, I looked outside from the window of my room at the short box-trees which had recently opened in the little garden of our yard.

We were sitting on the floor on the beautiful handmade carpet which my grandfather had bought for me exactly the year that he passed away, on my birthday. I stared at the sky and sunset which had covered itself with quiet little clouds.

I thought the wind was blowing up in the sky somewhere, although down there any footsteps of wind could not be seen. The wind wove the threads of the clouds like the filaments, just like every other phenomenon in nature such as seasons and the mild and stormy waves of oceans which have a certain and fixed time and arrangements. I knew that whatever happens inside us also moves on according to specified rules. I knew that the universe has been created in a beautiful way, but that evening the world had become more beautiful for me than anybody else.

The colors of nature were spread around me more elegantly than before and the light buoyant in the air seemed more sincere.

That evening Monir and I wanted to go for a long walk. We stepped out into the quiet blue evening. We went to a most beautiful forest which was not far from our house.

We started a very small fire in order to sit beside it for a while. A few steps farther, I gathered some pieces of wood. I then put a small piece of paper under the wood and lit it. A tiny smoke went up to the sky. It seemed that the smoke was hoping to get released. The red flame of fire was shaking strangely before the light of sunshine. The sky was smiling to me happily, the air was dancing flowing on anything. I picked a lily of the valley flower from the nearest meadow and I sat on the grass. I unfolded the small ground sheet which we had taken with us on the ground. Immediately Monir showed me a butterfly that came and sat on it to rest.

Monir was humming her favorite Christian song that we sang in almost every single meeting. Monir always said that every time she sang that song, she sang it with all her heart and always a great feeling of victory and joy was created in her heart by singing that particular song. After a while our small fire was out and gradually the sun had set.

At sundown always, when I hear the sound of the leaves in the trees, I like to walk and pray. If someone listens carefully to the sound of the leaves in the trees for a long time, this eagerness reveals its meaning. But my eagerness has always been an eagerness for God, for my memories in Christ and the new meaning of life in my Lord.

Every road leads towards a lodging and every step is a new birth in the living God. The Lord whispers his most beautiful and wonderful plans in our ears. If we have learned how to listen to the Lord, then our thoughts and mind begin to move on with braveness. All this happens very quickly. A person who has learned how to listen to the Lord does not mean to live just a normal and usual life without knowing what God's will is in that life.

The voice of the Lord leaps from one world to another world and the waves of his love and peace trickle to the ends of the earth. The freedom-loving voice of the Lord sings the most beautiful songs of the newborn ones and his healing hand is flowing everywhere, to heal the ill ones spiritually and physically.

The whole universe becomes one with the freshness and the deep meaning of God's love; all the hearts become joyful and unburdened.

Time is flying so quickly and we must go on by preaching the name of Jesus Christ. Preaching his name and transferring eternal peace and the new birth that he has placed inside me is my most important responsibility. If I have come out of the dark world of Islam and am not imprisoned in the prison of law and rules anymore, then I have actually taken steps towards light.

"Lord Jesus Christ is the greatest sunrise with a world full of forgiveness mercy, peace, and love."

During the whole night that Monir stayed in our house, we spoke about Jesus Christ. She explained for me how she finally understood that the only way in her life was Jesus and how she was led to him . . . how she had tried his sweetness and finally how she had seen God by her side all the time.

Because Monir was also born in a fundamentalist family, we could easily understand each other and we could share our feelings because we had almost the same troubles.

I explained to her the fear that sometimes came inside me and made me question if I was wrong. But I told her how much meeting Pastor Soodmand was helpful for me and how much better I had understood the meaning of salvation by his teachings.

That night Monir also explained the dangers that a converted Muslim might face. But I actually did not mind the dangers in that period of my life.

I told Monir that I wanted to pray that God shows himself more than before to me. Monir, who was a wonderful help for me to find out more about the greatness of God, closed her eyes and lifted up her hands. I did the same and Monir told me to tell God anything I had in my heart with a loud voice: "LORD, BEING MUSLIM HAS BEEN CHOSEN FOR ME WHEN I WAS BORN. I WANT TO LIVE ACCORDING TO YOUR TRUTH NOT MY PARENTS' DECISION. SHOW ME THE TRUTH OF LIFE. JESUS, YOU ARE THE WAY, SO SHOW ME MORE OF YOUR LOVE AND YOUR GREAT WAYS AND I WILL SERVE YOU FOREVER."

Then Monir read John 8:12 from the Bible:

"I AM THE LIGHT OF THE WORLD. WHOEVER FOLLOWS ME WILL NEVER WALK IN DARKNESS."

We were both very tired, so we slept very late. The day after was a big day for me and I was going to be baptized in the name of Lord Jesus Christ. I wanted to be completely ready for that big moment.

That very night I had a dream. I will never forget that dream and the prayer that Monir and I did. I was lost in the Sahara Desert. I had no shoes on and I was really very thirsty. I was frightened. Sunshine and darkness were both mixed. I could not recognize if it was day or night. I was running desperately when suddenly I heard a very loud voice who said:

"I AM THE WAY AND THE TRUTH AND THE LIFE. NO ONE COMES TO THE FATHER EXCEPT THROUGH ME."

The voice was so loud and strong that I jumped out of my bed while I was still repeating that sentence.

I noticed that I was standing and Monir was looking at me. She was still awake and she said that she had been praying all night long for me and never had slept. The way that I had jumped out of the bed she understood I must have had a dream, so she asked me about it. I told her my dream while I was crying. I told her that Jesus showed himself to me in that dream and I told her about the sentence that I heard so loudly in my dream.

She hugged me and while we were both choked with tears, she took the Bible and read exactly the sentence that I had heard in my dream. Then I understood that sentence was one of the verses in the chapter of John. I understood that verse was in John 14:6. I actually learned that verse from my dream for the first time before I knew that it was written in Bible. Monir, who had prayed for me all night long, prayed the last prayer and we both went to sleep.

In the morning we were both very tired but I was still thinking about the dream that I had. That dream had washed away all my doubts and all my fears and I never felt any doubt or fear again in my life. That dream had actually brought lots of joy and rest into my heart.

In the morning Monir was very excited about the baptismal service that we were supposed to go to in the evening. One of her classmates in the university was going to get baptized too. Her classmate was also a Muslim. Monir explained how she had given her a Bible in the university. Monir was very active in her Christian faith and she used to distribute all the Christian materials and the Bibles which she received from Pastor Soodmand.

That morning Monir said that she had to go to the university to pick up some books. She was supposed to come back for lunch and in the evening we were planing to go to that meeting. I thought that I would stay at home all day so I could go to that meeting in the evening.

Monir said that she would be back by one o'clock. In that morning I went to my room and I prayed and read some parts from the Bible that Pastor Soodmand had asked us to learn carefully. I was completely prepared to get baptized in the evening.

It was about two o'clock but Monir had not come back home yet. We ate lunch, but it was very strange that she had not shown up yet. She was always very punctual. Something must had happened to her. We were worried about her, so I called their house to see if she was there, but her father said that he thought she was going to stay at our house. They also got very worried when I told them that she did not come back from the university since morning when she had left the house. Her father said that Monir always calls when she is late so something must have happened to her. We started calling the university, different hospitals and everywhere that we could think of.

It was too late to go the baptismal service even if Monir came right at that moment. We had called their house and other places, and her parents were very worried and angry, so there was no way that we could go to that baptismal meeting. I was very sad that I missed the opportunity to be baptized on that day in that small apartment. I thought that everybody who was there in the meeting in that hour and others would get baptized except me.

I remembered that I had Ali's phone number. I could call him and ask if he knew anything about Monir. But the problem was that I could not call Ali in front of my parents.

My brother-in-law had already come to our house with his parents. They also had called everywhere. My brother-in-law said that when he had called to the university, they had said that Monir had not even shown up in the university that morning although she was supposed to be there.

My heart was beating so fast that I hardly could breathe. Monir's mother was crying hard and the least that we could do was console her. Suddenly the doorbell rang. We all looked at each other and we all thought that it must be Monir. After my father opened the door, we could see it was Monir's oldest brother who was a judge in the courts of Teheran. He came in, with a red face and very angry. Suddenly he said that Monir has been arrested!!!

Suddenly Monir's mother shouted and asked, "Why? Take her out of prison." But her brother said that she has been attending Christian meetings. While he thumped angrily on the table which was placed beside the door, he shouted *"Kafar!"* which in Persian means someone who denies Allah, an infidel or a nonbeliever in Islam. He was furious. As soon as Monir's mother heard the word *Kafar*, she lifted up her hands and shouted, "God kill me." I was frightened. Her father went into the kitchen and my mother started to console Monir's mother again.

I was very, very afraid of the word *Kafar*. I had to call Ali and let him know what had happened, but I was even afraid to make a phone call.

My parents did not let Monir's mother go home until late that night. They did not want to leave her alone by herself in that situation.

That night was the most fearful night of my life. That night I remembered how much Monir and I had prayed together the night before. I was choked with tears. I could not believe what had happened.

I went to my room and was crying so hard. I did not know what to do. I kept asking myself why all those things should have happened exactly the day after Monir stayed overnight in our house? After a night that we had prayed so much and I had that beautiful dream.

I remembered Monir's look when I jumped out of my bed after that dream and saw Monir that was still sitting and praying.

She said that she had been praying the whole night and never slept. I remembered how much she had prayed for me while she was awake and I was sleeping. All that happened exactly the day that I was supposed to get baptized—the day that I was praying and waiting for that long.

After Monir's family left that night, the cries of Monir's mother were still blowing in my ear. That night I felt Monir was with me there in my room and smiling.

I was trying to pray and ask God for help. I opened the same Bible that I had found in the library to read but as soon as I opened it, I saw a piece of paper with Monir's handwriting on it. She had encouraged me by writing a few words and had written from Colossians 3:13-14. I thought the night before when she was reading the Bible and praying, probably she had written that note for me to read later.

I just could not believe what was happening. I could not believe the fact that Monir was arrested. I thought how sorrowful she must have been under arrest. What Monir was doing in prison had stolen all my concentration. If they were hurting her in there, I really did not know what to think or do any more.

She always spoke about trusting in God. I was sure even in those days of prison, she was trusting God and was not fearful of anything.

That night I did not sleep even one minute. Early in the morning before everyone else woke up, I called Ali. His wife answered the phone. Her voice sounded worried and sad. She said that Ali was not at home. It seemed she did not want to speak on the phone. After I insisted that I had to speak with Ali, she said that she could not speak at that moment. She told me to stay at home and that she would call me shortly. After a while she called me from a public phone in the street and said that Ali was arrested. She said that their phone was under control by the Islamic authorities and explained that Ali had not come back home yet. She said that the fundamentalists wanted Ali for some questioning and had not let him go after the hearing. That had happened exactly the day after Monir had disappeared.

Ali's wife knew everything. She told me that the fundamentalists had come to their house and had taken many Christian materials and Bibles from Ali's house. They also had found the phone book where Ali had written all the phone numbers of those who were attending the meetings. My name and phone number were also in that book.

Ali's wife warned me that I was also in danger and my name and phone number were in Ali's book which the fundamentalists had found and taken with them.

After speaking to Ali's wife, my fear was doubled. I was even afraid of my own parents, the society and everybody around me. I had only one person who could help and protect me from everything which was going on . . . one person in my heart who was nobody but JESUS CHRIST.

One day after noontime, my mother and I went to Monir's house to find out if they had any news from Monir. Monir's oldest brother had visited her in the prison that morning. He said that it is really a shame for the whole family to have a converted sister in the prison.

My brother-in-law asked me if I knew anything about Monir before that happened since we were so close together. When he heard my negative answer, I saw in his eyes that he did not believe me.

After a few days of fear and agitation, Monir's father said that Monir would be released in two days. But he had given his word and had promised to the Islamic authorities that Monir would repent from her deviation and become a Muslim again. It is a Koranic rule that the deniers (*kafar*) must repent in the name of

Allah and Muhammed. Then they would be forgiven of their apostasy.

Because two of Monir's brothers were priests, it would make sense that they had made an exception for Monir—of course, only in the case of her repentance.

I was so excited to see Monir again, but I could hardly believe that Monir would repent. Actually I could not say what would happen. I did not know if I were in Monir's place in prison—under so much pressure—what would I do? Because Monir was a girl, for sure they had hurt her more during the arrest.

Monir's mother had planned a big celebration for the day that Monir would be released and come home from the prison.

Fifteen years ago in the national news of Iran on TV they used to announce a list of those who had been executed by shooting and the news commentator always named them "SEDITIOUS ONES."

I remember that day so clearly when my father as usual turned on the TV to hear the news. In the middle of the news, the commentator started to announce the list of those who had been executed by shooting particularly in that morning.

In the prisons in Iran, it is the rule that those who are supposed to get killed must not see the sunrise and actually must be dead by the time of sunrise. Anyway, after two or three names were announced, suddenly we heard the name which we were waiting to get released after two days. Monir Shams.

I was ironing when I heard Monir's name. The iron fell down from my hand on the floor. My mother, who was performing her *Namaz*, ran in to the sitting room. It is not permitted by law to stop *Namaz* in the middle unless it is a matter of life and death, but it was actually a matter of death.

They had killed Monir. I could not stand on my feet anymore.

My father said with a shocked face that they were supposed to release Monir from prison the day after. It must be for sure a similarity of names.

My mother was very anxious. She did not know what to do. In a few minutes we got into the car and my father drove in a great hurry to Monir's house. As soon as my father parked the car in front of their house, we already could hear the voice of Monir's mother who was shouting and crying. My father was wrong; there was no similarity of names. They had killed Monir.

Monir's mother was shouting and her voice was shaking the whole street which their house was on.

I was standing beside the car and was so shocked that I could not move my feet. I still could not believe what had happened. I was with Monir the last night of her life. How much we spoke about the future. She explained about her future and her plans after her studies. She was only twenty-eight years old with a world full of memories and hopes. All those dreams had disappeared with Monir herself.

My mother came and took my hand while I was still standing beside the car and was deep in my thoughts. I had not dared to go inside the house yet, but my mother and I went together.

It was such a heart-breaking view that not only I but nobody else, even the greatest writers, could describe it in words. Monir's mother had scratched all over her face and she was completely pale. Everybody from the family and relatives were there but only some of them were crying bitterly because most of the relatives were Islamic priests. Probably they all thought since Monir was converted from Islam that she was worthy of death.

I had never seen my brother-in-law cry before. I did not know what he was thinking when he was crying. I wanted very much to know what was going on in his heart at that moment and I was wondering if my grandfather was alive that day, what would he say about Islam?

The darkness of that night was heavier than other nights. The shouts and screams of Monir's mother were so horrible that I was never so afraid before.

I remember every moment of that night. It has always been reviewed like a movie in my mind every time I think about my past. Monir's mother, who was behaving very strangely, suddenly went to my father and while she was still racked with tears, said, "I want my Monir back." She ran into the room and brought the case that she had prepared with Monir's clothes and veil to take to prison the day that she was supposed to be released.

As she was holding Monir's veil, she was crying and asking everybody, "Where is my only daughter to wear this?"

That view was so heart-breaking that when I want to write down what exactly happened, even after so many years, my heart shakes and I have tears in my eyes and I cannot keep my hands from shaking while I am writing.

It was a heart-breaking night. I had sat down in a corner on the floor. A great fear surrounded me. I was not that brave to be able to deal with all my fears within me.

Monir's voice was still humming in my ears. I kept asking God and myself why should all that happen exactly after the night that Monir stayed with me in our house? She was the only one with whom I could share anything. But she was gone. My best friend and my sister in faith was gone.

Monir's mother was still shouting and asking everybody, "Where is my only daughter? I never let her before to stay out this late. She must be back. She must be back." She was truly shaking everyone's heart with her questions and words.

Their house was very crowded. I was thinking if I could tolerate the same penalty that Monir went through.

I had to find someone to get help from. While I was still sitting in that corner, I had hidden my head in my hands and asking God for help. Suddenly I felt someone's hand on my shoulder. There was standing a girl whom I even did not know. She gave me a piece of paper. We did not speak even one word. I just got the paper and went to the bathroom to read and see what the note was about. I did not know why I went to the bathroom to read the note.

It was a short note on which was written: "Leave the country as soon as possible. You and your husband's names have been revealed as converted Muslims. The Islamic authorities have all your names and addresses. All the ones who were attending the Christian meetings and were converted in Christ's name are in danger. Call this number." There was a telephone number written on the note. I memorized the number and when I came out of the bathroom, I had already destroyed the note.

I started to look for the girl who gave me that note, but I could not find her. She had disappeared. I looked everywhere even outside the house in the street but there was no sign of her. I never found her and never saw her again and I never found out who she was.

My husband and I were afraid to make any decision but we had to. In my heart I was feeling that I was about to leave my country which was not really my choice.

Traveling out of Iran was not a big deal for me, but escaping from Iran was not actually only a journey. I was losing my family and my country. Monir had suffered martyrdom and we really needed the Lord's guidance.

When we came home from Monir's house, I went to my room and sat on the bed exactly the place that Monir always sat. Only God knew how much pain had covered my heart and how much pain I had gone through.

I remembered that Monir told me a few times that NO MUS-
LIM IS ALLOWED TO CONVERT. THE CONVERTED MUSLIMS
WHO HAVE DENIED ISLAM ARE WORTHY OF DEATH.

A Muslim born is condemned to remain Muslim all his life.
There are those converted Muslims who got killed for their
Christian faith. Some of those martyrs are known and many
unknown. No Muslim is allowed to deny Islam otherwise would
be considered as infidel (*Kafar*) and is worthy of death. All the
infidels must be killed according to Islamic law. Of course, I
myself had read the verses in Koran which confirmed and sup-
ported slaying the deniers (*mortad*).

"THEY SHALL HAVE A CURSE ON THEM; WHEREEVER THEY
ARE FOUND, THEY SHALL BE SEIZED AND SLAIN (WITHOUT
MERCY)   Sura 33 (Al Ahzab) Verse 61

My husband and I were praying for the Lord's mercy on us. In
the morning my husband called the number that I had memorized the day before in Monir's house. A man answered the phone
with a Turkish accent. He said that he could help us escape from
Iran and move to Turkey. He said that in a secret way and did not
want to speak on the phone about it. He said that he could meet
us and explain more about everything.

Two more believers were planning to escape to Turkey
through that man, but he said that he would not tell us who
those two people were until we decided that we were following
them.

Our life was in danger and we had to escape to Turkey. It took
only two days before we decided to follow them to Turkey. That
was our only choice. The day that we called him to let him know
that we were following, he said that Reza and Bita were the ones
who were also escaping from Iran. Reza and Bita were two very
faithful believers who had come to Christ many years ago, almost
the time that Monir had given her heart to Christ.

Everything all around was happening so fast. The day after our phone call, we met the man who was going to help us escape from Iran. His name was Aman. He gave us all the information that we needed to know. He seemed so sure about everything and he promised that he would put us safely in the airport of Ankara. All we had to do was to be in the airport on Tuesday morning at 5 am.

I was so sad that I was leaving my country without even telling my own parents. But I even did not trust my own parents in those moments. Even my own family should not know where we were going. We could not trust anybody at all

Everyone of our relatives and friends knew that Monir had become converted and that was the reason she was executed. In the last days my brother-in-law, who was aware of all the information about Monir, had told my parents that they were suspicious that we were converted too. I knew that my parents, especially my father, was only waiting to become sure about it and as soon as he knew for sure, he would reject me as his daughter.

Shortly in a few days we would be leaving Iran. I knew that my parents would never forgive me for what I was going to do— for my Christian faith and escaping from Iran in such situation.

Although my father was a fanatic Muslim, he also had the kind of character that if I went to him and told the whole story and repented in front of him and also repented in front of religious authorities, he would have forgiven me and still provided for me more possibilities than before. But I, who had seen that dream and especially after Monir's martyr, could never again deny my faith in Christ. Seeing Monir the last night that she stayed with me in our house, staying awake and praying the whole night for me, had given me so much strength and courage that I could go through anything worse than the situation that I was in.

Although all my feelings were mixed and I did not know any more whom to love and whom to be afraid of, I still loved my parents and I was really tolerating the pain of leaving everybody around me.

I could not realize any more for what or which aspect of my life I had to be worried—especially after a test that I had with the doctor and he had told me that I was six weeks pregnant.

Everything around me had become like a circle of fear with all the sorrows and very serious and dangerous problems. Four days before escaping from Iran, we were still in my parents' house. They still did not know that we were leaving Iran.

In the last days I could not take my eyes off my mother's face. It was hard to accept the fact that I was not going to see them again. The last dinner that we ate together with my family, my mother asked me why I was behaving so strange. She said that I seemed so worried, but I told her that it was because of Monir.

My mother had almost become sure about our conversion, but my father was waiting for information from my brother-in-law who was in contact with the courts and prisons in Teheran. My mother still did not know what kind of danger we were in.

For the first time in my life, I understood what was the real meaning of fear. We were in danger in Iran; but I was so afraid of leaving Iran, on the one hand, and fearful of staying in my own country, on the other hand. We had to escape to Turkey; otherwise, soon in a few days we would have had the same fate that Monir went through.

On Saturday morning, which is the first day of the week in Iran, there was a letter from the prosecutor's office which two Islamic officials delivered to the door of our house. The letter said that I was requested to appear by the Islamic authorities and it was written that I had to be followed by my father.

That morning my father was at work and my mother, who had spoken with those officials, had opened the letter. I was upstairs and I saw my mother coming upstairs while was still holding the letter in her hands. She looked at me—a look full of sorrows and tears in her eyes—and said, "Why you? Why did you do that?" I, who was full of fear, did not answer anything and just said, "But now I believe much stronger than before in God." She threw the letter into my room on the floor and told me to stay in my room until my father came home. She said, "I cannot go through what Monir's mother went through." She left the room and left me alone with a world of fear and confusion.

I did not know what exactly to do, but I knew what would happen if I stayed any longer in that house. I knew that death was waiting for me in prison and I knew that if I went to the prosecutor's office with my father, he would come back home alone.

Three days later we were supposed to escape to Turkey, but our lives were already at stake. The same minute that I found out about the letter, I called my husband, rushed into my room and took a few clothes in a small bag. My husband told me to meet him in a street close to our house in order to go to stay in a safe place for those three days that were left.

I also called Bita to let her know what had happened. She told me to call her from the public phone in the street. We knew that all the phone calls were being monitored.

After the phone calls I made, I went downstairs. I did not let my mother see the small bag that I was going to carry with me. I saw her sitting and crying. She said that I was not allowed to go outside the door and leave the house. She was very much afraid of that letter. I knew that she loved me so much that she did not want anything to happen to me. I told her that I had to meet my husband and told her not to be so much worried. I told her that I had not done anything wrong and the letter was probably just for questioning from my husband.

My poor mother did not know what we were going through and she did not know whether to believe me or not. I wished I could tell her the truth, but I knew if I did I was in trouble and she would not let me leave the house at any price. She looked at me with eyes full of agitation and begged me to come back home soon.

I went out of the house with a small bag of clothes hiding in my hand and a heart full of sorrows and cries. While I was walking quickly in the street, I was choked with tears and was feeling so desperate.

I got a taxi to go to the place where I was supposed to meet my husband. When I called Bita from the public phone, she said that we could go and stay with them those three days.

Reza and Bita's apartment was almost empty. They had sold or given away all their furniture. They also had received a letter from the authorities and they were also summoned by the prosecutor's office.

In that period of time, the Islamic fanatics had captured and killed so many people who had just been sent the arrest warrant letter. The fundamentalists actually follow no rules or particular system in their actions and decisions, but I believed that it was only God who truly had mercy on us. Our names were listed among those who had received a letter from the authorities. Perhaps God knew that I was not so brave like Monir to go through what she went through.

Four of us stayed in the house of Reza's friend for the last day and night that we were still in Teheran before our flight. My husband and I were glad that at least we could stay with them during those days of fear and difficulties.

The last night in that friend's house, we all read the Bible and prayed for some long hours. We were going to travel the day after and only God could help us through that way which was full of dangers. If the fanatics had captured us in the airport, it was equal to death.

I was thinking about my mother. I thought how worried she was for me that I had not gone back home that day. I could not imagine what they were going through during the time that they had no news from us. Perhaps they thought I was captured by the fanatics exactly the way it happened to Monir.

We were standing at the beginning of very huge and intolerable experiences. We were leaving our own country in less than one day. A fight had started within me. A fight for survival.

I was afraid of getting killed. Getting killed by those who probably would hurt me a lot before getting killed. A power was drawing me out of my country and, in fact, leaving Iran was the only choice that we had.

The fundamentalists had captured and killed Monir so fast and unexpectedly. I am sure if Monir had seen or felt a tiny sign or warning, she would be alive today.

Through Monir's bravery and the zeal that she had for Christ and her faith, many other Iranians could be led to Christ and leave their hearts to him. But the fundamentalists killed her without giving her a chance and her name was registered in the list of martyrs forever.

I have learned the only way to victory in life is to be dauntless and to have no fear and not to become discouraged in the time of frustrations and failures because even the disappointments and frustrations will go away from the way of those who are courageous and have no fear within.

In that period of time, I was left alone in a circle of strong feeling, escaping from Iran and not knowing exactly what to do;

the whole of life actually meant nothing but staying alive.

But how to survive and how to go on were those issues that I had truly left in the powerful hands of Jesus Christ. I trusted strongly that the Lord would take care of us in the path of danger and difficulties.

I had learned strongly that victory is waiting for those who take steps and start to act and it really never waits for those who are conservative and timid and the ones who try first to deliberate the result of everything correctly and completely.

That last night in Reza's friend's house, Aman (the man who was supposed to help us escape) came and visited us. He spoke about the day after, the airport and all the details about the way. All we had to do seemed very easy to him when he was explaining.

Bita and Reza were very happy. My husband also seemed quite sure and happy, but I who was the youngest and also pregnant for the first time in my life was filled with fear and sadness. I had lost all my concentrations, all my joy and peace that I had gained through the last few months.

We did not sleep the whole night. We were counting even the moments to go to the airport in the morning. We were really lucky that we had found Aman who could help us escape from Iran, otherwise we would have had to escape through other borders which were a lot more difficult and dangerous.

About five o'clock in the morning, Aman came to pick us up. We were sitting in Aman's car. A cool wind was blowing through the window. I was crying the whole way to the airport.

I hated that particular early morning. Still after so many years very early mornings remind me of that morning driving toward the airport when I had to escape from my own country.

Bita was holding my hand and told me that soon we will be

back. I never believed her but I knew that it was better to fly far but stay alive.

Aman had his own contacts in the airport. We went through the entrance, but we were not supposed to pass through the same gate that other passengers were passing. We went to the back side of the airport.

I was afraid, tired and pale—so much that I did not know where I was walking to. I was just drawing myself with others without knowing where to. The signs of pregnancy had started in me and I was feeling bad because of my morning sickness.

An airport employee came to Aman and shook his hand and said, "I will take care of them." Aman said goodbye to us and we followed the airport employee to his car. I thought that any moment someone from the government would come and stop us. I felt much safer with Aman before he left us. I had no more energy to draw myself ahead.

The employee drove us to the airplane and in a few minutes we were in the airplane. My seat was beside the window. I was taking my last look at my country . . . the country which I was born in but then I had to escape from there. A great sorrow had conquered my heart.

I looked out of the window in the airplane. I remembered Monir's face. I heard her mother's cry and I remembered my mother's eyes which were full of tears, her anxious face the day that I went out of the house and promised her to be back soon and never went back. I remembered the humble and kind look of Pastor Soodmand when he preached Jesus' love and I remembered Ali who was still in prison and would probably be killed by that day.

I knew that my parents were looking for me everywhere by then. My head was going to blow with all those thoughts when suddenly I found myself crying.

The airplane was already flying in the sky and I, with a small bag and full of memories, were on the plane to Turkey, an unknown country. But I had fixed my eyes on the future and trusted the Lord to hold the reins of my life.

ESCAPING ABROAD

I did not feel danger any more while walking in the airport in Ankara. One of Aman's friends was supposed to meet us in the airport and help us to find a cheap hotel to stay.

The place that the man took us to stay, which he called a hotel, was actually a ruined building with a few small rooms. On the first floor a very old man was sitting behind a very old table with a sign of "Reception" on it.

We laughed when we saw that man with the sign of reception in that ruined building. The people who had rented the other rooms did not look like travelers. They actually looked like homeless people and drug dealers.

I had never been in such places before, but I was happy that at least I was not alone.

Turkey was not a safe country to stay very long. The fundamentalists were seen in the streets of Ankara. I still had lots of fears within me from them and I never felt safe there. I knew that the Islamic fanatics had their own activities in Turkey.

The day of our arrival in that room in that ruined hotel, we did not have anything to eat. Finally we went down the street to find something to eat. There was a Turkish grocery where there was a very nice and friendly man. We had very little money and we looked extremely tired because we had not slept for several nights. When the man saw us with some food that we had picked out in his store, he did not take money for what we had in our hand. He did not say anything except he just said that we did not need to pay. Perhaps he had seen Iranians like us before who had escaped to Turkey and had understood our situation. Although we saw him for a short time, his kindness during those days has remained in our minds forever.

When I escaped from Iran, nobody (even my own family) knew about it. I had not trusted anyone because I was afraid of everybody.

I was very worried about what my family had gone through during those days when I suddenly disappeared. Perhaps they thought that the Islamic forces had captured me and had killed me already just the way they killed Monir.

A few days after our arrival in Turkey, I decided to write a letter with no address on the envelope to my parents just to let them know that I was alive and also to let them know completely about my Christian faith even though they had found out about it already when I was in Iran.

I knew that all the telephone conversations and even letters were under surveillance, but I had decided to send that letter so at least my mother could be informed that I was alive.

Actually the Lord had put in my heart to write that letter. After so many thoughts in my mind about sending that letter, finally I took pen and paper and started to write.

I trusted the Lord, but I did not know how to start or what to write. I just remember when I started the first word, I went on for five pages. I wrote in the letter how I kept the Bible that I had found in the library and how I read it by that flashlight at night. I also wrote how Monir had preached to me and prayed with me and how I saw Jesus in my dream and about the Christian meetings that I attended for several months.

And finally I wrote proudly that I WAS A CONVERTED MUS-LIM WHO COULD HEAR THE VOICE OF THE LORD DURING MY PRAYERS.

Jesus had taken my hand and had taken me safely out of Iran. I did not mind anymore what they would feel or decide when they received my letter. I even thought that the Islamic authorities might find the letter before my parents, and it actually happened exactly as I had thought. The authorities found the letter and showed it to my parents and then kept it as evidence that I had written by my own handwriting.

There was no address written from me, so I felt safe about it except for the stamp on the envelope which showed clearly from which country the letter was mailed.

Jesus Christ had brought me safely out of my own country so I had to give my testimony to my family and I wanted them, especially my mother, to know that I was alive.

We had trusted the Lord that he would take us out of Turkey safer than he had brought us from Iran and still he would place us in a safer country permanently although we had no money and no support during those days.

We were surrounded by the light of the Lord and it was only the Lord who could open the doors to us as he has promised that he would do for his children. But I still carried the hatred from the Islamic forces and the fanatic ones who had killed Monir and had captured Ali and had caused all those disasters in my life. Through writing that letter I thought that I had confessed what I had to confess in front of the fundamentalists, so somehow I felt that I had found some comfort. I wanted them to know that even if they kill Christians secretly and torture them in their prisons, there are also those who God takes out from that dark country with his power and saves them from the lagoon of death.

Writing that letter had pacified me a lot, but we were praying day and night that the Lord would take us to a safe country from Turkey, to a country that he himself had planned for us until we could live more securely in that new land.

When I wrote that letter to my parents, I was sure that it was not only I who had decided to write that letter but I believed that it was the Lord who led me to do so. When I was writing that letter, my whole body had become like a piece of fire. After finishing writing, I put my hand on the letter and prayed much stronger than any time, put it in the envelope and in the morning the very first thing I did was mail the letter.

I had to mail it fast because if I waited perhaps I would have regretted writing it and probably I would tear it up and never mailed the letter.

There was no way that I could call to Iran; the phone was tapped and I was afraid to hear my father's voice. But I was very happy that I had mailed that letter. At least they knew that I was alive and my letter was actually a confession of my Christian faith and a confession of how Jesus Christ had saved me from that lagoon of death.

After a few days I was wondering if my parents had received my letter; I just had to call Iran. So I decided to make that telephone call. My mother answered the phone and told me the Islamic authorities had my letter and knew that the letter was mailed from Turkey. She said that my father was wanted by the prosecutor's office. They had shown my letter to my father and had kept it as a confession of my Christian faith that I had written by my own hand. My mother told me that my father had gotten a heart attack from reading the letter in the prosecutor's office. They had taken him to the hospital right from there and he had stayed in the hospital for a few days. What I was hearing was like a stroke on my head.

My mother was crying on the phone and said, "Why did you

write that letter? Why?" My mother said that my father had rejected me completely and had erased my name from his and my mother's identity cards in the registration office and had demanded that nobody in the whole family, especially my mother, was allowed to speak to me or have any kind of relationship with me.

She said even that minute that she was on the phone, she was speaking secretly. She wanted to inform me how serious the matter of rejection was.

I could not speak on the phone any more. I was crying hard when I hung up and so was my mother.

On that day any kind of happiness had subsided inside me, but still a voice from the bottom of my heart was warning and encouraging me not to give up and the same voice was telling me that the Lord had a great plan for me.

Since that day I knew that a stony wall of distance was built strongly between my country, my parents and me. By building that wall, all my hopes and dreams were washed away and destroyed—the dreams and hopes that anybody has in mind just to be able to go on in the valley of life.

But since that day every time I remember my parents' faces—with respect of all hope that I had in Christ and all the growth in my faith and all the intensive teachings that I received in the most difficult times of my life right in the middle of danger—I feel that my heart is in pain and my whole body begins to shudder . . . a shudder that is full of worry, fear, and love for them, feelings which even the most able and professional writer cannot put into words on a piece of paper.

Some spiritual conditions and thoughts that sometimes slowly and sometimes quickly move in one's mind had started in my mind. I had to review all those thoughts and feelings one more time and build up everything from the foundation and, until someone has been in the same condition, he would not be able to understand exactly what kind of situation that is.

A heavy stony wall of distance was established between my family and me, and it was completed by writing that letter. Of course, that wall had brought alot of worry into my mind, but I had learned that there is a price for everything in this life which must be paid. That wall of separation was the price that I had to pay for my Christian faith. Monir had told me several times, and even Pastor Soodmand had spoken about it, that the converted Muslims have to pay a very high price for their Christian faith.

Rejection from the family, giving up the dreams and life in one's own country and even death under the hands of dark forces would be that high price for converted Muslims.

The same day that I confessed in the name of Jesus Christ while pastor Hossein Soodmand was preaching and I became a Christian, I knew that sooner or later I would be rejected by my family. But rejection was not completed at that time because my parents did not yet know about my Christian faith.

My rejection was completed the day that I escaped to Turkey from that lagoon of death. My rejection was completed through the letter of confession, which was written by my own hand, confessing that I belonged to Christ. Not only had my parents read it but the authorities as well. Of course, I wanted only my parents to know about me, but it happened that first it was the Islamic authorities who had received the letter.

Many times I cried in Turkey. Sometimes I cried so long that my eyes became like a desert that had no tears to fall anymore. I cried so long that there were no more tears and no sign of life left in my eyes and then I stopped my crying when I realized I really had no more energy to continue.

For many years after those days in Turkey, still the voice of my cries hummed in my ears. I had never cried so much in my life.

During those days I was hoping that I could become filled so much with thoughts of the future that I would not think about my past any more.

My cries had slowly changed to whines that came from the bottom of my heart. Each day that passed brought more anxieties and sorrows to me. Our escape from Iran, our unsafe entrance to Turkey and my physical condition during my first pregnancy was exactly like someone whose leg is broken. At first you do not even understand that the leg is broken and you do not even feel the pain, perhaps thinking that a blow has been inflicted because the bone is still warm. But gradually, when the bone gets colder, you scream and cry from the pain and it takes a very long time until the leg heals.

We had escaped from Iran in order to stay alive. It was not really important which country we were in or how our life was going to be day by day. But in an unsafe and disorderly country like Turkey, the pain of our life was increasing and the feeling of insecurity was getting worse each day.

Every night we were praying that the Lord would open the doors and would save us from Turkey and all the fears and anxieties in that country.

I was in very bad physical condition, very sick. Rejection from the family whom I loved with all my heart—a family with whom I had spent all the years of my life, a family who had provided everything that I wished just to make me happy—was actually such a heavy pain that I could not accept it as I constantly remembered the beautiful and innocent face of Monir in front of my eyes and the voice of her mother's cries in my ears.

It was like yesterday that they had killed her. All the time my imagination did not leave me alone about how they had killed her, if they had tortured her, and in what kind of condition her body was after getting killed. I just could not stop thinking.

I had lost everything I had in my life but that was the price that I had to pay for my Christian faith. Instead I truly had learned to focus my eyes on the future and trust the Lord to hold the reins of my life.

I had completely lost my appetite. I was physically in pain and I had a high fever. My husband and Reza laid their hands on me and prayed for my health whenever we prayed, and it was only by God's power that I could go on with the illness which had started in me. We did not have money to go to the doctor or buy any medicine and only Jesus Christ the healer could heal me.

In that difficult condition, I felt that I had to speak with my mother. I had to call at a time when my father was not at home. I just needed to speak with my mother. I had nightmares and was scared to call home.

But one morning I decided to call Teheran and speak to my mother to see what her feelings were. The last time when she spoke to me about my rejection, we both had become so upset that we hung up and I did not know what she felt about the whole thing.

In the morning when I called, it was my mother who picked up the phone. As soon as I heard her voice, I burst into tears and said, "Forgive me, mother." She was surprised and did not believe that it was my voice. She did not know what to say but started to ask how I was.

My mother said, "I just want to ask you one question: How could you do all those things with the reputation that we have?" She could not believe how I could go through all those tragedies without telling even one word to my family. Then she asked me if I was still wearing my veil. As soon as she heard my negative answer, I did not hear any voice or any word from her but quickly I told her that I will always love her and asked for her forgiveness. She hung up without saying a word, not even goodbye. I did not know what her reaction would be when I called her in the future.

For many years since I was nine years old, I had worn the veil. In the beginning of my conversion to Christianity, it was really hard even for myself to take that veil off after so many years because wearing it had become part of me. The first day when I took it off , I remember that I was very shy to go out in the street. When we got to Turkey, I was still wearing the veil.

For I who had worn it from my childhood, it took actually some time to get used to not wearing it. Even Monir was wearing veil when she was speaking and preaching the word of God, so I never thought about taking the veil off after converting to Christianity. I was not really prepared to do that.

Wearing a veil was an unbreakable bond which had connected me to my past memories. Now that I wanted to take one step forward, that unbreakable bond had tied up my hands and feet. I knew completely that I was captivated by past traditions.

Man must keep some bonds related to the past and even protect them, but wherever those bonds are hindrances or are imprising us in tradition, they must be broken and discarded.

Sometimes traditions have wonderful things inside them, but sometimes they become like heavy and fearful chains which make our growth extremely difficult.

Wearing the veil was a tradition that had captivated me since I was nine years old. It had become part of me like my hands and my eyes. Wearing it was so precious and valuable to me, just like my eyes, that taking away it from my life was like a sighted man who was going to lose his eyes. Continuation of life would be almost impossible for that person.

Sometimes I felt that I could not continue living without wearing the veil. I thought that wearing it was as important as being sighted, but I decided to break it off and put aside that rusty chain of tradition so I could live freely.

My Lord had established a trust inside me that I could go to his presence simply and I learned that wearing the veil did not clean my heart and my inner being. When the shutters are closed, inside becomes dark but everywhere outside light and sun are luminous. If we close the trapdoors of our eyes, it does not mean that the light outside has been destroyed.

When I left Iran I thought it would be for a short time. I had not realized that there was no return in the way that I had chosen for my life. Fighting to survive had stolen all my concentration and I really did not know where that way would end.

Life was terrible and very difficult in Ankara. We did not have enough money to eat and to live. In the room where we were living, there were all different kinds of insects. The days were intolerable for me and we had to stay most of the time inside our room.

One day I had missed my family so much that I asked Bita, "Is it possible to go back to Iran some day?" Bita took my hand and said, "Don't even think about it. Why don't you understand? There is no way to go back again. We have escaped from that country, and the fact is we can never go back again."

The same day that I had that conversation with Bita, at nighttime we prayed a lot. During the prayer Bita cried very much. We had spent a few weeks together then and we knew each other very well, so I asked Bita why she was crying so much. I told her that she could speak to me and we could at least pray together for what was bothering her so much.

That night she explained to me about her past. She said the reason that she was explaining her past was that she wanted me to understand that there are those who have been in worse situations than I so I could feel a little bit better. Because I was taking notes of whatever was happening in those days, she asked me if someday I wrote a book about my life and my faith, to write about her life story and the difficulties that she had gone through in very young age and her childhood. I, who was broken-hearted myself, listened carefully to what she had in her heart to say.

Some years ago Bita's parents were on the way to the north of Iran in summer time when they were in a serious accident on the road. Both of them died right there in the car. Bita was only six years old at the time. Her father, who was a very wealthy man, had mentioned his brother's name in his will. Immediately after the accident Bita's uncle put his hand on his brother's wealth which, of course , was according to the will of Bita's father. As is the rule in Iran after the death of both parents or even one of them, the custody of the children belongs to the family of the husband. Bita and her sister went also under the custody of their uncle who was a selfish and stingy man.

Bita's uncle used those two sisters as servants to do the housework in that big house which actually belonged to Bita's father. Their uncle did not allow the two sisters to go to school. But Bita and her sister, who loved to study, used to hide old newspapers in the kitchen and they practiced reading and writing the words from those old newspapers. The whole time of their childhood was spent working as servants in that big house until Bita became seventeen years old.

Bita was a beautiful and noble young girl who was always witness to her uncle's parties. Many times he got so drunk that he started to beat her and her younger sister for no reason.

One day Bita's uncle said that his partner, who was also a very rich man, would come to their house because he was interested in getting married to Bita.

Bita's uncle told Bita that he had already agreed to their marriage; otherwise, their partnership would fall into trouble. One time that Bita had started to disagree with her uncle, her uncle had slapped her face so hard that one of Bita's ears became deaf from that time. After that slap she became silent since she knew if she spoke anymore, her uncle would beat her more.

She had become silent and had actually left her life in the hands of fate. Her uncle even set up the date that his partner was coming to their house to speak about the marriage date and all the details. Her uncle had said that same day Bita would have the chance to meet her future husband.

On that particular day, when Bita and her uncle were waiting for the man, Bita's uncle had said that he had to leave the house to do something that was an emergency but he would be back before his partner arrived.

Bita was so disturbed that she even considered running away while her uncle was out . . . but running away to where, to whom? Besides she knew if her uncle found her, he would definitely kill her.

Finally after so many thoughts that came and went into Bita's mind, she stayed at home waiting impatiently for her uncle to come back as he had promised. But while the thought of running away was still on her mind and also the thought of what would happen if her uncle's partner came before her uncle arrived, suddenly the doorbell rang.

Bita, who was already fearful and disturbed, had opened the door. It was Hossein, her uncle's partner. Seeing that man, a great fear surrounded her. Hossein had asked Bita if her uncle was at home and, when he heard that there was no one at home except Bita, in a few minutes he rushed in and attacked Bita. He hurt her and immediately left the house.

That night when Bita was explaining about her past, she was shaking and tears were falling down her cheeks just like a river. I asked her not to continue, but she wanted to go on. She said that she would feel better when she spoke about it.

After Hossein left the house, Bita, who was scared and hurt, hid herself in the corner and was crying. After sometime her uncle came home and saw Bita in that condition and heard what had happened. Not only did he not believe her because he thought Bita had made up the story in order not to get married to Hosssein, but he also decided to punish her. So that night, after so much pain that Bita had gone through, her uncle had started to beat her harder than ever.

Bita, who was already in pain from being beaten by her uncle, became like a half-dead body when she went into her room. After one month, when Bita was feeling bad, they found out that she was pregnant. Then her uncle understood that what Bita explained about that day was the whole truth. By then it was too late for everything.

But because her uncle himself was also a roguish man and Hossein was his partner, he did not want to jeopardize their big investments and financial relationship by dicussing that event. Bita's uncle not only kept quiet about the whole matter but also forced Bita into marriage with Hossein, the man who had attacked her before the marriage. Because Bita was pregnant, the marriage had to take place very fast although that life did not last more than five years . . . five years full of bitterness and getting beaten almost every day. Sometimes Hossein had beaten her so hard that Bita found serious problems with her health.

The result of Bita's pregnancy was a boy who lived with Bita only the first five years of his life. Bita's mother-in-law also used to live in the same house where they lived. Her mother-in-law always took the child in her room and never let Bita be alone with the child.

Bita's son was actually growing up with his grandmother which was, of course, what Hossein wanted. Bita, who had become just a servant and an instrument for her husband, finally decided to run away from that house. She could not take her son with her because her mother-in-law was always with the child and never let her take the child outside. For this reason Bita decided to run away to an unknown future even though it meant she would never see her dear son again.

Bita could not stop crying during the time that she was explaining about her past. She insisted again that I must write about her life in a book that I was planning to write and trying to take notes for at that time, but a shadow of sadness covered her face. She still wanted to continue to say how finally Jesus Christ had saved her from all those difficulties, illness and darkness and how Christ had healed her spiritually and physically.

Sometimes words are not able to describe man's within, and Bita's life was one of those lives which man can hardly find the right words to explain about.

Bita, who was many times beaten by her uncle in childhood and then her husband in later life, was almost paralyzed in her right leg. She had to use a stick the time she ran away from her house. Every day she had so much pain that she asked for her death a hundred times a day from God. She cried every day and asked God to save her life without even knowing what she really meant by the word of salvation.

After she ran away from the house, she went to an old friend to stay with her for sometime until she could figure out what she was going to do.

The apartment which Bita's friend owned was in the same building that Ali and his wife were living in, but none of them knew each other. One afternoon when Ali had gone to the apartment of Bita's friend to borrow a screwdriver, Bita opened the door. When Ali saw Bita's condition and the pain that she had with her leg and could not even walk properly, immediately he asked if he could pray for her.

Ali had entered the apartment and, without even knowing Bita, had started to pray for her. Then he went to his own apartment and then came back with a Bible in his hand for Bita and preached to her about Jesus, salvation and the Lord's healing with such courage and faith.

Bita explained that after Ali had left she felt such a wonderful peace and relief in herself and in her friend's apartment where she was living. After a few days, when Ali had a meeting in his place, God had put in Ali's heart to invite Bita too. Bita had gone to the meeting. She explained how much she had cried in the meeting and asked God to save her life. Bita gave her heart to Jesus Christ right in the first meeting.

Ali and some others had put their hands on her and had prayed that the Lord heal her leg. After the meeting Bita went in the street to walk a bit. She had her stick in her hand. After walking a while, she was so deep in her thoughts that she fell down on the ground. Her stick was thrown to the side. She laid on the ground and could not move. She was worried how with that paralyzed leg she could reach her stick in order to be able to stand up again.

It was late at night and there was no one in the street to help her. There she realized that only Jesus Christ could take her hand and make her able to stand again. In the meeting that she had given her heart to Christ, she had heard how Christ could help and take her hand. So right there, while she was still lying on the ground, she started to pray with all her heart. Her voice was shaking and tears had made her face completely wet. She prayed with a loud voice, "Jesus, help me; help me to stand up. I know that only you are able and have the power."

After she had prayed, although she thought that she did not know how to pray, she had felt a very strange strength in her body. She tried to stand up and she did it by the power of Christ. At the first moment that she was standing, she could not believe that she was standing there with no stick in her hand. Although she had given her heart to Christ just a few hours before, she did not doubt. While she was filled with the Holy Spirit, she was standing on her feet and praising the Lord that he finally had taken her hand and had healed her. Bita, who had been lying on the ground and worried how to reach her stick with that paralyzed leg just a few minutes ago, in that moment was standing on her feet and was praising the Lord. She was filled so much with the joy of the Holy Spirit that she even did not go towards her stick to take it home with her.

That stick remained there forever, and Bita went home with two healthy legs and no stick in her hand. Since that night she never felt any pain in her feet. The Lord healed her completely. While she was explaining to us how the Lord had healed her that night, she had her hands lifted up and was praising the Lord who had cleaned all the effects of paralysis from her feet. Bita wanted to emphasize very much that it was Jesus himself who had put his hand on her leg and had healed her.

I, who had shrunk in a corner in the beginning of Bita's story, suddenly noticed how eagerly I was listening to her by saying "Amen" and "Hallelujah!" I could not imagine how many difficulties she had gone through in her life.

Hearing Bita's life story about how much God had changed her life brought lots of blessing into my life. That night I had almost forgotten about my own sorrows and I just had opened my mouth in praising the Lord.

Hearing Bita's life story renewed my spiritual energy, and I understood that there are always those who have lived in more difficult situations than the person himself and absolutely have gone through more difficulties.

That night I promised Bita that I surely would write down about her story if I wrote a book because I was always taking notes of my life even in the most difficult times. Because my grandfather was a writer and he always took notes wherever he was, I also had learned from my childhood to do the same.

In the last days of staying in Turkey, the Lord had poured his peace so much in me that it seemed nothing dreadful had happened in my life. I knew that by escaping from Iran and leaving my family, I was rejected. Especially by writing that letter and confessing my conversion to Christianity and denying Islam, the seal of rejection was stamped on my parents' hearts and also on my Iranian document and actually my whole life.

A fact of my life was that there was no return to my father's land. I had started a way and there was no way of return in it. Turkey was also a land of insecurities, although we were at least secure from the Islamic officials of Iran. There was still lots of chaos going on and Islamic fundamentalists could be seen in the streets of Ankara. Every day of our life was being passed in fear and in secret.

It was only the Lord who had given us strength and courage to continue and go on with our life. We had to do something quickly. We were praying day and night that the Lord would help us to get out of Turkey just the way he helped us escape from Iran. Very clearly we saw the hands of the Lord that took our hands and took us out of Iran. I was praying that the Lord would take away the fear and stress within me. It was only the Lord who could take us to a safe country where we could live safely and be witness to the name of Jesus Christ freely with no more fear.

We had to move to a safer country than Turkey as soon as possible, but I had not thought of leaving Turkey. Even though we were afraid of the authorities inside Iran, I still did not want to get very far from Iran.

For the first time after the last night that Monir was alive and stayed in our house and prayed for me, again fear had come to me. I also had become very sick physically.

For the first time after my Christian faith, I asked myself, "Why did I ever get involved with the Christians? Why did I get involved from the beginning?" Sometimes I even condemned myself for being born in a Muslim family. I actually had lost myself and my control. I could not realize anymore what was right or wrong, and I was confused for what aspect of my life I was worried.

I was missing my mother. Everytime I remembered her look the last day that I left home without saying anything to her, it was killing me. My heart was in pain when I remembered her face.

I decided to call Iran again and hear her voice even though she had hung up the day that she heard I had taken my veil off. I called Teheran and, while I was hoping that my mother would answer the phone, suddenly I heard my father's voice. He sounded more serious than ever. I did not dare say anything and sadly, without even thinking about it, I hung up.

That day I had become much more sick than the other days. After I hung up and came out of the public phone to go to our room, I was going up the stairs when suddenly I felt very dizzy and suffered a blackout. I fell down the few steps that I had gone up and I did not understand anything after that.

When I opened my eyes, I saw I was in our room and my husband and a Turkish nurse were also there. I understood that while I was on the stairs, I had miscarried the baby I was carrying. I was in a lot of pain and, in addition to the physical pain that I was going through, one more spiritual pain was also added to my other pains. I had lost my first baby because of the stress and fear that I had been going through during the last few weeks.

Although I knew my mother was very angry with me, I felt that I had to speak with her, especially after miscarrying my baby.

My mother was also very fanatic about her Islamic faith because, if she was not, she could not actually live with my father so many years. Even so, she never let her religious belief stop her from loving her children—especially me who was her youngest child. I had to realize that she herself was also one of the victims in the history of Islam. My husband also insisted that I call my mother. He said probably I would feel better by speaking to her.

I called one more time without knowing who would answer the phone this time. As soon as I heard my mother's voice, I was really relieved. By hearing my voice she understood that I was very sick. When she heard what had happened to the baby, I heard her crying on the phone. I understood that she still cared about me. She said that she had not rejected me in her heart although the rest of the family did. She was always such a encouragement for me. She said that she was very happy and praising Allah that I was at least alive after all had happened and at the end of our conversation she added, "How can I reject my own daughter to whom I have given birth?"

I will never forget how happy I was after speaking to her. At least there was someone who still loved and cared about me. My husband and Bita also became very happy when they saw my smile.

The whole time we stayed in Ankara took about seven weeks. Because of the risky situation we had, we could not go out very often. We spent lots of time reading our Bibles and every night we prayed for several hours and we had already started fasting. We trusted the Lord with all our hearts and knew that it was only he who could save us from that situation in Turkey.

The affects of miscarriage were still in my body. I had pain and fever but we had no money to go the doctor. But that Turkish nurse helped me somehow with very basic medication.

What I had gone through was a lot more than my capacity. During those seven weeks in Turkey, God taught us many precious lessons right in the circle of those troubles. There I understood that man learns the most wonderful lessons right in the middle of difficulties.

It was not very long after I had given my heart to the Lord but everything had happened so fast. Monir had suffered martyrdom in a very short time after we had prayed in the name of Jesus Christ in my room, and it was still very hard for me to believe that she had been killed and was not among us any more.

For many years I could not speak about Monir. Everytime I wanted to speak about her and her faith and my spiritual experiences with her, a heavy-hearted silence conquered my words, and it took truly some long years until the Lord healed all those pains.

In the beginning when I had become a Christian, I heard that many people think that the Old Testament is related to the old days. But how clear and well Job's life spoke to my heart when I read it many times in Turkey during the most difficult days of my life. I actually understood the real meaning of life with a completely new vision.

In those difficult days of Turkey when I had just lost my first baby because of my fear of life in Turkey and I had become rejected by my own family and all the sorrows of our unknown future, it was only the power of the Lord and Job's life and his experiences that kept me on my feet. Every time that I started to read Job's life, my tears started to flow down from my eyes.

When Job's sons and daughters were feasting and drinking wine at the oldest brother's house, a messenger came to Job and said, "the oxen were plowing and the donkeys were grazing nearby, and the Sabeans attacked and carried them off. They put the servants to the sword, and I am the only who has escaped to tell you."

While he was still speaking another messenger came and said, "the fire of God fell from the sky and burned up the sheep and the servants and I am the only one who has escaped to tell you."

While he was speaking another messenger came and said, "the Chaldeans formed three raiding parties and swept down on your camels and carried them off. They put the servants to sword, and I am the only who escaped to tell you."

While he was speaking, yet another messenger came and said, "your sons and daughters were feasting and drinking wine at the oldest brother's house when suddenly a mighty wind swept in from the desert and stuck the four corners of the house. It collapsed on them and they are dead, and I am the only one who has escaped to tell you."

At this, Job got up and tore his robe and shaved his head. Then he fell to the ground in worship and said:

"Naked I came from my mother's womb, and naked I will depart. The Lord gave and the Lord has taken away; may the name of the Lord be praised." (Job 1:13-21)

Job's life comforted me many days in Turkey, I saw clearly how the realities of Job's life still happen in today's life.

In the beginning of my faith, I always praised the Lord that I did not know what would happen next in my life. Otherwise, I am quite sure that I could never go through all those difficulties during the escape from Iran. I also praise the Lord that he chose me to give my heart and be one of the witnesses of his love and his cross inside my own country, Iran.

God did not choose only the prophets but all those who come to him to fulfill different missions. Those Christians who got martyred in Iran, including Monir, fulfilled their mission. Preaching the word and love of God was the most important mission that they had—preaching to many Muslims including me who were imprisoned in the dark and tall walls of Islam.

It has also been my permanent prayer to be able to go on with whatever the Lord has planned for me. It has been my prayer to be a zealous soldier for the name of the Lord, to be able to stand in front of people and shout proudly what Jesus did in my life and how I got saved from darkness and death.

Of course, there were times that I became very weak and got scared of what was happening. Sometimes I really hoped that whatever was happening was nothing but a dream, that I would just wake up in the morning and find out that whatever had happened was a dream that I had the last night.

Everything had happened so fast that sometimes I could not believe the days that we were in Turkey. On the other hand, in the most difficult times of danger and loneliness, I could so clearly hear the voice of the Lord who told me: "NOTHING IS IMPOSSIBLE FOR HIM."

No matter how hard life would become or how deep we are in the circle of dangers, the Lord always surrounds us with all his power and love and He takes care of us with his marvelous and wonderful miracles if we leave everything in his hands and follow his will.

Teheran has always been my dreamy town, the town of my memories . . . the town that has always been placed in the center of my heart. Every day in Turkey I reviewed the small fellowship group we had that was full of the Holy Spirit. But fear of getting killed and struggles to escape from Iran and trying to stay in faith had erased all those beautiful memories of my town off my mind.

Sundays had become very holy for me. We had wonderful meetings on Sundays. I could speak to my Lord in my mother language. I could pray in Persian which meant lot to me. Someone who has prayed in a foreign language all his life would understand what a great gift it is to pray in one's own language . . . a great gift that I had paid a high price for, but I could tell simply to my Lord what I had in my heart.

Moving on to an unknown future was taking me even father from my memories. The great and unique peace that the Lord had poured in my soul had changed me completely to a new person. I who was always after God with eyes full of tears and searching for him with groans and regrets through *Namaz*, fasting and Islamic law, was changed to a person who felt the presence of the Lord constantly beside me.

In the beginning of my Christian faith, a big question mark was made in my mind. Does God truly reveal himself so easily to anyone who believes in him? When I asked Ali, the leader of our meeting, this question, he said that of course the Lord reveals himself so easy and clear to anyone who believes in him with all his heart. God is with those who leave behind anything and anybody just for the name of Jesus Christ and carry on his cross every day and go after him.

I had read the Bible many times in Iran and I always asked Ali my questions. He always answered them with patience and humility. Sometimes I felt that he was busy and tired, but he always took his time and explained carefully whatever I and others asked him.

I had become very close to my Lord. I could hear his voice so clearly that every time I prayed alone or in our meetings my whole body started to shake. And still in Turkey, with all the worries and fears which were inside me, I could pray for hours. I truly learned in Turkey how to spend time with my Lord. Every time I prayed, I felt his wonderful presence beside me and the tears of joy made my face wet.

Of course, sometimes great fear and sorrow surrounded me and I became very afraid, but right there my heart became full of joy and hope. The Lord had anointed me so much that I did not think any more about Iran and all those difficulties that I had gone through in the last few months. I had found the true meaning of existence that man has struggled to gain from the beginning of creation until today.

Many books have been written, so many lectures have been made and so many wars have been started just in order to reach that prosperity and the true meaning of being. So many crimes have been committed, but through none of them man could reach that final and eternal prosperity.

I have observed myself how some people search for happiness in wealth, in position, in temporary pleasures, in power and finally in science and knowledge. They spend all their life to reach where they have in mind. But as soon as they get there, they see that they are the poorest and have been running all their life after nothing.

I had found a special relationship with the Lord which was not only deep and close but also assured. Having a direct relationship with God was not a dream anymore but it was the reality that the Lord himself proved to me that it was true through his presence and his miracles.

I have learned not to trust my feelings and emotions because my feelings and others' change constantly. The environment of life, health conditions and even the weather can change man's feeling. Man is an uncertain created being who is subject to changes by temptation and different feelings. That is why my spiritual growth has never depended on the changes of my feelings or my emotions at all.

From the day that my whole body became like a piece of fire and I stood up in our meeting and yelled, "I want to have Jesus," a revelation had started inside me which is impossible to describe in words. That relationship became stronger through my baptism that took place in another country which you will read about in the next chapter.

As a converted Muslim I was like a blind woman who had found her sight. I will never forget the day after my baptism when I woke up and opened my eyes. I remembered that I did not have to pray toward Mecca two times in the morning, eight times in the afternoon and seven times in the evening in Arabic which was not even my language. Mecca is a place which is covered by a black curtain and no one knows what incidents were passed behind that black cover and what crimes were accomplished.

What a relief it was that I could pray in Persian, my own mother language anytime and anywhere. Through Jesus Christ I felt such a relief; I could breathe better and easier. For so many years I was in a dark jail which God himself had become my jailer.

What a relief that I could fast any day I wanted and I did not have to fast only during the month of *Ramadan*. My fasting was the time when I went to the presence of the Lord with all my being. If I fasted, others did not have to fast by force. Christians fast for the Lord in order to spend more time praying and cleaning their hearts and souls, not to show off or be noticed by others.

God does not need my fasting. If I fast it is for my faith and my spirit. God does not need my prayers and my good deeds or anybody else's. I actually understood the fact that God cannot be bought by my good deeds.

What a relief to be free from all those rusty chains of law! I was so joyful and calm in my Christian life and in Christ . . . exactly like someone who gets lost in an unknown desert and, after so much searching and going deviated paths, suddenly finds the right way.

When I found Jesus, I felt such a relief and I could breathe better. For so many years I was imprisoned in the chains of law that God himself had become my jailer and suddenly I had become free. I could smell freedom in all the areas of my life.

As a Muslim I was like a lost person in a desert who is thirsty and the continuation of his life depended on a gulp of water and suddenly finds a water-well.

In my Christian life I have always heard the voice of the Lord when I pray and strongly feel his presence everywhere I go.

I am a converted Muslim who is a born-again Christian now. I am born again in my soul, in my spirit and in my heart. I am so much changed since I became a Christian. Fear has no meaning to me anymore and I have so much peace and rest inside me.

During my Christian faith I always have had such a pure joy that I cannot describe even a bit of it. From the beginning of my faith I have loved Jesus Christ so much that I have always been ready even to die for his name just like Monir and all those Christians who got killed for his name.

In those days in Ankara, Jesus was so close to me that he had become the most important one for me. I could easily hear his voice that he spoke to me through his word.

My Lord was not that dreadful God any more to whom I always went with fear and always suffered to become accepted by him. My Lord was not a hard-hearted judge anymore who always condemned me. My relationship with him was trustful and I dared to bring up and confess my weaknesses in front of him. I did not have to cover and hide my weaknesses and my sins through my good deeds.

The voice of my Lord is full of love and rest—a voice that never was heard before when I was a Muslim.

Although I always performed my *Namaz* and I did it so carefully that it took hours behind the closed doors and I cried and concentrated on the words of my *Namaz* and even the cassette of Koran was played and I could hear the Koranic verses by my whole heart, I never felt the presence of God. There was no spiritual confidence in me and I was not sure if my prayers were accepted or not and I did not know where my prayers were going.

I remember the first night after Pastor Soodmand prayed for me and I confessed to my Christian faith in front of Christ and him. I was so much filled with the Holy Spirit that I was crying like a little child. I felt so much joy and acceptance for the first time in my life that the Lord Jesus was my personal savior. He had become so close to me that I felt I was the only one that he died for. I had received so much power inside me that I was ready to tell everybody about my conversion from Islam. I wanted to tell the whole world about my testimony.

When I escaped from Iran, I had the feeling that I would be outside of the country for a very long time. In that time I just wanted to escape and it did not matter to where or how we were escaping.

Then again we were on our way to another country from Turkey. We had no idea what would happen in the new country. We just remembered that wherever we went we could be witnesses of the Lord.

I had started to tell everybody I met how I had become a Christian and why I was converted from Islam. I did not mind if anybody got upset or did not want to hear me out. I did not want to keep silent anymore about my life. I could not be silent about my salvation or what we had gone through when I was a Muslim. I wanted to tell my testimony to the whole world of what God had done in my life.

Everybody around me had heard my testimony except my own family—my loving family to whom I did not even say goodbye when I escaped from Iran . . . the country that I was born in and where I grew up and went to school . . . the country that all my beautiful memories belonged to. Just because I did not want to be a Muslim any more, I had to leave everything behind and escape not only from my country but from my whole life and my whole wonderful memories. I preferred to run away with a Bible which I had found in the library rather than to let the dark forces make me keep silent.

Then every time I opened my mouth to pray, the Holy Spirit filled me so much that I could not sit down and pray anymore. I had to stand up and shout that I loved my Lord and that Jesus had saved me. I was filled with the Holy Spirit. How could I be silent in front of the power of God? How could I be quiet in front of all those miracles that I had seen in my life by my own eyes? How?

During the last days in Ankara, when I woke up one morning, my husband and Reza were not there in the room. I went out of the room but could not find them. I had become very worried for them. Because the Turkish government and the Iranian government cooperated together, they had an agreement not to let the ones who had escaped from the country stay there. They must be captured and sent back to Iran.

I had become very worried and did not know what to do. We could not go outside in the streets very often and that day I waited until noon, but they did not come back.

I remember that day we were all fasting. I did not know to whom or where I could go if something happened. I was sitting in the room and staring at the door hoping that one of them would open the door shortly.

In the evening when I was almost sure that something had happened to them, suddenly Reza opened the door. I could not believe I saw them again. After what had happened to Monir on the day that I waited and waited for her and she never came back,

I always had bad feelings when I waited for someone.

I was very angry and upset, but Reza and my husband were very glad. They said that they had been looking for someone who could help us to move from Turkey to a safer country and finally they had found such a person.

I actually became glad that we were leaving Turkey because I was getting sicker and sicker every day. We could leave all those difficulties behind in Turkey. The next night the man whom my husband and Reza had met came to our place. He said that he could help us to move from Turkey but, of course, the risks were there, too. He mentioned that weekends were the best time to fly out of Turkey. That Turkish man had contacts and friends everywhere and he knew all the police officers in the airport.

The seven weeks that we spent in Turkey were like seven years to us. We thanked and praised the Lord for the doors that he actually had opened to us. The last day that we wanted to leave Turkey I really was wishing that Monir was with us. I was missing her a lot.

I thought that our dream had come true that we were leaving Ankara. Five days later we had to get ready to go to the airport. I remember it was an afternoon when we left that ruined room where we had lived for seven weeks and went to the airport. We were supposed to meet the man in the airport.

After waiting about thirty minutes he came. While we were waiting, I wondered what would happen if he did not show up at all. He asked us to follow him without asking any questions.

We did as he told us, but this time, just like the day that we wanted to leave Iran, I did not have confidence. I was pale and hardly could draw my feet after my body. I was almost shaking and could not control myself. I was still sick and my body was sweating as I was walking. The man, who was helping us and had noticed my behavior, asked me to control myself.

The man helped us go past the officers in the airport. As we passed through passport control, he said a few words to the officer who was sitting there to control the passports. He knew that officer very well and they seemed to be very good friends. The man was speaking to the officers with his eyes and they understood each other very well.

Finally, when we were at the gate with the boarding cards in our hands, he shook my husband's and Reza's hand and just turned his face to Bita and me and said goodbye. He said that was all he was supposed to do for us and then he left us at the gate. Still scared and unsure what would happen next, we rushed to the plane.

The memory of escaping from Iran was one more time reviewed in my mind. All that fear and stress came back again to me, and the memory of losing my first baby was killing me.

We were on our way to another unknown country—Spain. That was the only country where the man could send us. It did not make much difference anyway because we had no money, no experience in different countries or even knowledge of what was the best thing to do. We just wanted to move to a safer country and be immune from the dangers of our own country.

We were finally in the plane and were sitting in our seats.

I had started to turn over the pages of my life. Jesus Christ had taken care of us until that moment. Although I was very sick, the melody of joy was starting to play in my heart again. I was missing Monir very much in the last few days. I hoped I could see her one more time and tell her how proud I was of her and tell her about the wonderful results which I achieved after all the difficulties that she went through to help me to know Christ.

I wish she could see how strongly I had known Jesus and his power so that nothing and nobody could separate me from him.

I was very deep in my own thoughts and tears were running down my face when suddenly on my shoulder I felt the hand of the stewardess who was offering me chocolate!!!

IN THE HEART OF MADRID

In the airport in Madrid, we waited for Bita's friend who had lived there for many years. She was supposed to come and take us home. Shirin was one of the converted Muslims who had come to Christ many years ago. While we were waiting, suddenly Bita saw her friend Shirin standing at the information desk looking for us. As soon as she saw us, she ran to us. Bita and Shirin hugged each other and she hugged me too just like she knew me from before. Shirin was a very nice and friendly girl.

When we got to Madrid, I had a fever and was sicker than the time I was in Ankara. I had really forgotten what happiness meant after all those difficulties in Iran and Turkey. We were all very tired. For a few nights before our flight, we had not slept at all.

When Shirin saw that I was so sick and had a high fever, she said that we had to see a doctor as soon as possible. She called a taxi so we all could go to her apartment.

On the way home I looked at people who were happy and were walking in the streets freely. I could not believe that finally we had fled to a country that was a lot safer than the country where we were before. I was feeling quite secure.

Shirin told the taxi to stop in front of a very nice building. When we got out of the taxi, I took a deep breath and I truly smelled freedom. I really had not tasted freedom for a very long time, especially after what happened to Monir.

Shirin and two more girls were living together. They had rented a big apartment. Shirin had cooked dolma for us. We were very hungry—especially after seven weeks when we had had nothing to eat in Ankara except bread and cheese and perhaps warm food a few times. By the time we wanted to eat, although they saw that I could hardly stand on my feet, they all asked me to pray for the food. I truly praised the Lord for his presence with us through all those difficulties and dangers that we had passed through.

After dinner Shirin's roommate came. She had her Bible in her hand. As soon as I saw her, I thought what a blessing that she could carry her Bible so freely in the street. When we were introduced to her, she started to explain about the meeting that they had in the church that night.

She was very happy that she could be in the meeting that night. Shirin did not know about us. She just knew that we were in Turkey before we moved to Spain. Shirin said that it would be a great idea if we could go together to the next meeting of the church. The meeting was open to everyone. It was the first time that we would be attending a meeting that was open to everybody.

The pastor of the church had heard about our arrival so he sent one of the sisters in the church to take me to the hospital. I finally met a doctor after some weeks of illness and got the necessary help that I needed.

After Monir's martyrdom I had serious problems sleeping at nighs. The first night that we had arrived in Madrid, I could not sleep at all. One time in the middle of the night, when I again could not go to sleep, I went to the livingroom and I saw Shirin who was still awake reading her Bible.

I remembered Monir the last night before the day that the fundamentalists captured her, when she stayed in our house overnight. I had had that dream about Jesus and, when I woke up, I saw her still awake and praying for me. Everything around me reminded me of Monir.

That night, when Shirin saw me standing there, she asked me to sit down so we could speak and, since we were both awake, we could pray together.

In the morning my husband told me to call my mother in Iran and let her know that we were not in Turkey any longer. Probably she was very worried about my situation. I did as my husband said. My mother actually was very glad when she heard my voice.

Whenever I heard my mother's voice, I could not control myself. My tears were falling down on my cheeks, especially when my said that she was not allowed to mention my name in the house and nobody in the family should understand that my mother spoke to me on the phone because I was rejected by the whole family. But she insisted that I must not become sorrowful or give up. But how could I not?

Through my conversation, Shirin had found out what was going on. She had become very upset, but she did not speak even one word about it after that conversation with my mother. The same day that I spoke with my mother, at two o'clock there was the meeting in church.

In the heart of Madrid, at two o'clock we were standing in front of a very old building with broken stairs. Then we entered a large room. About thirty to forty Iranians were sitting in the room and there were a few Europeans, too. They were already praying by the time we got there.

Among the people who were sitting there and praying, a tall blond gentleman was sitting there who had a very trusting and kind face. After the prayer he started to speak in Persian so fluently that it was unbelievable that he was not Iranian because he spoke that language so fluently and perfect. He had such a sweet accent when he pronounced some of the words. The pastor was a man of God and a man of prayer who preached very strongly. After the prayer they started to sing some happy songs while the pastor started to play the organ.

I loved the song "Jesus comes with all his glory." They were clapping their hands when they were singing. Great joy I could see in their faces when they were singing. I thought of myself and those who had worshipped God all those years in our Islamic faith with tears and sadness.

Their joy really reminded me of all the years that I was a Muslim and I had worshipped God with eyes full of tears and a heart full of fear. It also reminded me that the seventeen times of prayer each day in Arabic and all that fasting in *Ramadan* not only did not open a ray of hope to me but also caused me to lose all the ones who I loved.

The topic which the pastor was speaking about that day was "God is love." For me and others who were from Muslim backgrounds and knew Jesus as a prophet all our life during our Islamic faith, hearing those messages were very important. Adam, Noah, Moses, Jesus, and Mohammed were those five prophets whom we respected as Muslims. Of course, we believed that Mohammed was the last and greatest prophet of Allah. Although I was only seventeen years old when I became a Christian, that day I felt such a pity for myself because I wished I had known Jesus Christ at an even earlier age. I thought that I missed a lot for not knowing Christ earlier than age seventeen.

The message that the pastor gave was a very strong and powerful one. The Lord really spoke to my heart after hearing that message and after what we had gone through.

After the meeting the pastor came to us. Faithfulness and kindness were shown clearly in his face and everybody could feel that without even knowing him because he had very special love in his face.

I did not know what to call him so I called him "father." I thought perhaps it would be more polite to call him that, but he smiled and said that I did not have to call him father.

That day we spoke briefly about Iran and Turkey and whatever we had gone through, about the fellowship that we had in Iran and we explained to him how the whole group was scattered.

After the meeting a couple who lived close to the church invited us to go to their home. While Ahmad, the man who had invited us, was offering tea in his apartment, he started to give his testimony about how he had become a Christian.

He showed pictures of the day that they had gotten baptized. I told him that he was lucky that he had become Christian out of Iran so he did not have to go through the difficulties that other Iranians who had become Christians in Iran went through. He said that he understood completely what I meant. Suddenly he had tears in his eyes when he explained that his brother had been killed just one month before in Iran. He did not know the exact date that he was killed. He mentioned that his brother led a Christian fellowship in north of Teheran. Immediately my husband, whose face had become very sorrowful, asked what the name of his brother was.

As soon as we heard the name of Ali, we were all transfixed in our places. Ahmad's brother in Iran was the one who was leading our meetings in his apartment. Although we were sure that he was the same person, we asked Ahmad if he had any picture of his brother Ali.

When we saw Ali's picture, we saw that he was the same faithful soldier of Jesus Christ who preached in the meetings in Teheran . . . the same man who had preached to Bita and many others. Ahmad's tears fell down on his cheeks and he started to cry.

Ali, who used to answer our questions and preached to us and prayed for us, had encountered the same fate as Monir during the time that we were in Turkey.

I remembered Ali's face—how happy he was when he sang in the meetings, and I remembered that he always said that every day of his life was a meeting with the Lord. And now we learned that after we had left Iran, Ali got martyred in prison.

Ahmad said that he knew that his brother after his martyrdom was with Christ and it is only that promise which makes him happy for Ali. Ahmad said he did not actually cry when he heard the bad news from Iran

We, who were very sorrowful ourselves, encouraged Ahmad and admired him for his strong faith. I truly wished that I had such courage to stay in Iran and die for Christ's name in that country.

On the weekend the church had a picnic. Going to a picnic in the wonderful weather of Madrid in those beautiful parks was really pleasant. On Saturday morning we all met in the most famous park in Madrid, La Casa de Campo.

All the members of the church were like a big family. They cared about each other and they had really learned how to listen to each other and others through the teachings of the pastor of the church. For me, who had grown up in a fundamentalist society, that simple picnic meant a lot. Everybody had brought something to eat. They put all the foods together on the table and after prayer everybody started to eat.

Sometimes it is very important and useful to use just the simple examples of daily life in order to analyze the most difficult and deep aspects of life. Referring to heavy documentary materials does not always help people; most people cannot even understand them.

After lunch our pastor, my husband and I had a long walk. I explained how I had found my first Bible in the library and about Pastor Soodmand when we confessed in Jesus' name in his meeting and Monir who got martyred and Ali who was Ahmad's brother who we had found out in Spain was martyred in prison. I shared with our pastor everything I had in my heart. We were very broken-hearted and that pastor really had the gift to listen to us—not only to us but everybody around him.

The Lord had anointed him so much for serving his name. He was quiet but full of intellectual aspects. I told him that I was still carrying the fear that I always had inside me. I told him that when I wake up in the very early mornings I still think for a moment that I have to do my *Namaz* and also the feelings of *Ramadan* were still in me.

Right there while we were walking, he stopped and started to pray for us loud, clear and full of the Holy Spirit.

The day that we entered Spain, we had absolutely nothing with us except one small bag in our hand. We did not even have enough clothes to wear in addition to all the problems with my sickness. I only had two t-shirts; everytime I washed one of them, I had to wear the other one. In the beginning the pastor of our Iranian church helped us with anything he could. Sometimes I thought about how rich I had been when I lived with my family in Iran; but in that period of life, we had become completely poor.

Of course, I praised the Lord that I was among the children of God. I praised the Lord even if I had to wear others' clothes that belonged to Christian believers.

During those days we were very much in need. Our food was bread and cheese and sometimes canned food. The best food that we ate was bread and potatoes.

I have a memory from those days that I will never forget. Once we had nothing to eat—absolutely nothing—and we had no money to buy anything. We only had two potatoes, so I placed them on the stove to cook and we decided to pray while they cooked. We were so deep in prayer that we forgot about the potatoes. The water in the pot was gone and the potatoes were completely burned. We stopped praying as the smell of burning spread in the apartment.

Regretfully I looked at the pot of potatoes which had turned very black inside. We were very hungry and we had to find something to eat. Many times we had gone to our pastor's house when we were in need and he always had helped, so we were ashamed to go there again and say that we had nothing to eat.

The only thing that I had brought from Iran was a very expensive miniature that my grandfather had given me on my birthday. That was the only precious thing that I had with me and that miniature was my only memory from my grandfather.

We knew a Spanish family who was almost our neighbor. Whenever we went to them, they insisted that we had to stay to eat with them. That night we were so hungry that we decided to go to their house, but we were embarrassed to go just like that so we decided to take a gift for them.

That beautiful miniature was the only gift that I had to take for that family. I was sure that they would invite us to stay for dinner. Although that miniature was very precious to me, it was the last thing I could think of. Because I had already lost many important things in my life, one miniature did not mean a lot. In addition, I thought the lady of the house would be very happy for that gift from Iran.

We went to their house and they were very happy to see us. I gave them that beautiful miniature and she was very excited to see that gift. Unfortunately we found out that they had already eaten their dinner before we got there. They were washing the dishes. The hope of having some food with them was gone, and we were too shy to say that we were that hungry.

They invited us to drink coffee with them, but we were so hungry that drinking coffee was the worst thing in that moment. But, because we were hungry, we were too shy to say anything. We drank that coffee and did not say a word to them of what had happened that night.

By the time we left their house, we had forgotten how hungry we were, so we slept that night hungry but with prayer and thanksgiving to the Lord. We were just glad that we did not know what would happen next in our life.

The next day was Sunday so we went to the church. It was the most important day of my life. For the first time in my life, I went to an official church on Sunday morning which was open to everybody to attend. There was even a sign outside to inform passersby of that service.

After a few beautiful happy songs, the pastor started to preach about forgiveness, which was an issue that I needed very much to hear about in those days. I had not really forgiven in my heart those who had killed Monir or my dear brother Ali. What I was hearing was wonderful. About half an hour later, a very special kind of joy filled me. I can never explain in words what kind of feeling it was. A wonderful and strong power from inside me was making me open my mouth.

As soon as the pastor read from the Bible, "JESUS SAID, FATHER FORGIVE THEM, FOR THEY DON'T KNOW WHAT THEY ARE DOING" (Luke 23:34), I stood up and shouted, "I want to have this forgiveness. I need your peace and rest more, Lord."

My heart was beating fast and tears fell down on my cheeks like a waterfall. The pastor and a few more had come to me and put their hands on me and prayed.

I was feeling the presence of the Lord so strongly in that room. I actually was feeling the warm hands of Jesus Christ on me and I felt secure in his hands. I had found my peace and rest one more time. A great power of forgiveness had come inside me. And the most important thing that happened to me, I felt that I had nothing against those who had killed my best friend and sister Monir and my brother Ali.

That day after the meeting, when we went home, I went to my room and I started to speak with the Lord. I had spoken with him many times before but that very day was quite different.

Jesus Christ had given me back the joy and assurance that I almost had lost after Monir's martyrdom. I truly heard the voice of the Lord that night. After all those disagreeable months, my real connection with the Lord was reestablished again. I thanked and praised the Lord for the relationship that I had found with him, the relationship that I was looking for all my life.

We had not gotten baptized yet. Because of all those happenings in Iran and our escape to Turkey, there was never any chance that we could get baptized. So a week after what happened in the church, we asked our pastor to baptize us; he accepted gladly.

I wanted to be baptized in the name of that God who forgives, who I can pray to in my mother language, whom I can go to when I need him and he would answer me whenever I said, "JESUS, I NEED YOU; TAKE MY HAND"—the one who is my father not a fearful judge and the one who does not condemn me all the time.

The day I got baptized was a beautiful day. The pastor had

already told me to give my testimony. I had written down what I wanted to say. I tried to make it short, but the moment I stood in front of the members to share what I had prepared, I took the paper and put it aside. I started to say what the Lord was telling me. The Lord was actually leading my words. I felt Jesus Christ beside me and I had no more fear within me.

We were thirteen people who got baptized that day. The moment that the pastor took my whole body under the water and pulled me out, I was born again. I was completely a new person with a new vision.

I must say that my faith actually grew up in a small poor church. The city hall had warned us that the building was too old and the fellowship must find another building. We were a poor church where the collection plate was always empty because most of the members were like us and did not have any money to give to the church. The members could hardly afford to pay their bus ticket to come to the church.

Yes, a poor church but full of Holy Spirit. Full of God's miracles. How proud I am of that small church where my faith grew. . Our pastor was not only a pastor who led the Sunday services and other special services, he was actually a father for all the members, a friend, an adviser and the one who had to think about all of our difficulties. He was a man who I am sure many times went through very difficult days in his life but gave his living money to help with the needs of the members. The remembrance of that wonderful church and the pastor who was truly man of God will remain forever in my mind as well as all those who came to Christ through him and grew up in that church.

After traveling the narrow and dark way of religious law, Jesus Christ broke all those old and rusty chains that I had carried since my childhood. The Lord had healed my broken heart and had made me his child . . . I who was born in a world of *Shariat* and had grown up in a world completely different and separated from Christianity. The Lord had melted me and my character with the fire of Holy Spirit and had burned away any kind of pride and selfishness inside me.

I was always proud of my grandfather's and father's reputations and wealth. Whenever I went to the university with my father, everybody looked at us with respect and it was always such an honor to walk with my father in the university. Suddenly I was alone with no money and no food in a foreign and disorderly country like Turkey. But I learned to pray and praise the Lord constantly even in the cold and difficult days of Turkey when we had nothing to eat.

I had felt the Lord's presence beside me and learned to hold his victory flag in my hand. I had learned not to run away from difficulties and troubles but to stand firm and fight. I had learned that times of difficulties were times of healing.

The Lord had healed inside me and my heart. He had filled all the empty spots of my heart with his love. He had filled my emptiness and the empty spots of my heart with his joy and peace. Although I was poor in that period of life, I was rich through his wonderful hopes and his own spirit. I did not have time to think about the past any more. The Lord had healed my thoughts so much that even if I wanted to remember a memory from the past or the difficult days in Iran and Turkey, I had to think hard to remember them.

Victory never waits for those who are timid and reserved, those who always want to measure the result of every thing exactly. I have learned the only way to success and victory is to be dauntless and not to get discouraged in the difficulties and in exhaustion. All the defeats go away from those who are brave and walk in the name of Christ and do not let fear inside them.

In my Christian life there were some series of unbroken

chains which made me related to my past. Every time I planned
to take one step ahead, those chains wrapped around my hands
and my feet and made me captive to those old thoughts and traditions. I tried to keep some of those connections with my past,
but wherever they were hindrances to my faith and my life, I
broke them and threw them out. Of course, many times spiritual
and emotional battles happened in those times inside me.

My faith and the vision that Christ has placed inside me does
not deserve that I look at my past all the time. I have deliberated
my past with all my faith and the Holy Spirit that is inside me. I
have admired whatever was admirable and I have locked whatever was not from Christ in the prison of traditions and threw out
the key to that prison in the deep ocean water..

My eyes are concentrated on the future and my steps go forward. I have learned to look at the future instead of the past.

The shutters of law are closed to everybody who follows
them. Everywhere has become dark, but out of those shutters of
law, there is light everywhere. If the followers of law have closed
the shutters of their lives, it does not mean that all the light has
been destroyed and gone. Most of the time that is the biggest mistake in our life because we do not use our senses completely. We
have not even learned to use our ears and eyes to see or to listen.

The Islamic rules and law are necessary for the fanatic rulers
to be able to rule over them and have easier domination in the
society. The most important mission of the Islamic rulers is to
spread and preach the law which even they themselves do not
obey and live by.

Man learns many different experiences from others, but an
experience is precious when it is gained by man himself. There
are those who, although they have lived long years, think and
behave like children and cannot decide or distinguish the life
itself.

I do not prefer those who read many different books rapidly in a short time. I think they just look at the books and finish them the next day. There are many books which are not even worthy to read and so many ideas and ideologies that are not worthy to be examined.

There are western writers who have written some hundred-page books about Islam and Muslim's life and there are those writers who have written about the converted Muslims and their spiritual and family conditions. But writing about a nation or certain religion without knowing the feelings and culture of that religion or nation is not meaningful.

In order to write about a nation like Muslims, the writer must know that nation or the followers of that religion completely. The writer must be steeped in Muslims' thoughts and must have felt what they feel and understand what they create.

If a writer writes about converted Muslims, he is doing a more difficult job. The writer must have known the roots of changes and the conversions and must have benefitted from all those analyses.

I believe the writings of those who have spent only some years of their lives searching and studying Islam would be very weak. When they publish their hundred-page books, they are only a collection of theories because they have not even lived in a Muslim country with Muslims for many years in order to feel what the Muslims feel in their private lives and what exactly they go through in their childhood.

The real value of spiritual and intellectual changes are hidden in the lives of those converted Muslims who have given up all their lives and have come to Christ.

Which writer who has not seen and felt those kinds of lives is able to describe that high price that each Muslim has to pay when he or she denies Islam? Which writer can really describe the faces of those who stood up to pay the price of their faith which was martyrdom? Or the spiritual conditions of the families and children of those who were killed for their faith? Only those who have gone through those persecutions themselves can understand and write what persecution means.

WHY AM I CONVERTED?

Tasting freedom was pleasant. I knew that the distance between God and me was because of the chains of *Shariat* and the chains of law all those years—years that I was lost in the dry wilderness of Islam. Then I knew that looking desperately for a way to freedom was over.

"I AM THE WAY AND THE TRUTH AND THE LIFE."

John 14:6

The verse that I had learned the first time from my dream came to mind again. One more time I was born, but this time no one had the right to whisper the confession of Islamic faith known as *Shahada* in my ears when I was a newly born baby.

"ASHADU AN LA ILAHA ILLALLAH; ASHHADU ANNA MUHAMMADAN RASULU LLAH."

"I witness that there is no God but Allah, and Muhammad is the messenger of Allah."

I was filled with Jesus' love and he had cleansed my heart from all the fear, hatred and bitterness. My permanent companionship with fear had made it even sometimes a familiar channel to me.

A Muslim spends all his life praying and concentrating on the world after death. Fear is part of Islamic life and prayers. At four o'clock in the morning, I had to wake up and do my *Namaz* because I was afraid of not doing it, because I was afraid of Allah. Everybody who confesses who is a real Muslim must first perform the *Shariat;* if not, he has not fulfilled his Islamic faith.

Doesn't God understand prayer if it is done at other times of the day? I was supposed to buy Allah and his blessings through my good deeds; I was supposed to buy his satisfaction through my good deeds so that I might not be burned in the fire of hell.

But after I was born again and got baptized, I could freely pray to the Lord anywhere and anytime and in my own mother language. Jesus Christ had opened the gates of joy to me by saying, "whoever drinks the water I give him will never thirst. Indeed, the water I give him will become a spring of water welling up to eternal life." John 4:14

My joy in my Lord had no limit. Jesus Christ became so close to me and healed me and became the most important one to me.

Shariat was the mirror that showed me my sins, but Christ was the one who *saved* me from my sins. Jesus' life itself was actually the strongest support for his teachings. When he said, "I am the life," he raised Lazarus from the dead after four days.

After my baptism I felt joyful and proud. I told about my new life to everybody and started to grow in my Christian faith and life. I learned to trust God in times of both happiness and sorrow.

I have always spoken to my Lord simply in my own words. No matter how loudly or silently I prayed, he always heard me and I always felt his warm hands on my shoulders.

The unique treasure that I had found was not just a prophet who died and stayed in the grave forever. I had found Jesus who conquered death and was resurrected after three days. This unique treasure was Jesus Christ the son of God.

During my Christian faith, whenever people from my own country and other nationalities have met me after I have introduced myself, they have always immediately asked me why I became a Christian. They wonder how somebody from a Muslim family background has become a Christian. They want to know all the details and reasons why I am converted. They want to hear convincing reasons why I left my Islamic faith behind and became a Christian.

Many times I asked that question myself. When I was alone in my room with my Lord, when I was in the middle of difficulties and have swallowed my sorrows in a secluded corner with my Lord, I have asked myself why I have become a Christian. That question is the reason which made me write down only the most important reasons why I chose Christianity. Otherwise, if I plan to write down all the details that I studied and searched during my Islamic faith, it would be a complete book by itsself.

I, who was born in a fundamentalist Muslim family and grew up in a fanatic family, have felt the frigid world of Islam. After seventeen years living in a fundamentalist family, I had learned and knew exactly what Islam and *Shariat* meant. I know that world of fanaticism is a world of darkness. In order to answer to all those people who ask me about my conversion, I decided to explain some of the most important reasons for my conversion and also to explain the blackness of the Islamic religion and law. I feel I can express these feelings more clearly through this written word than I may be able to speak them.

My only goal is presentation of all the realities that I myself struggled with during my Islamic faith. I do not intend profanity. I just intend to explain how the religious law led me into captivity, a law which imprisoned me in the prison of contempt as a woman. But Christ released me from all those rusty chains of law and religion and placed me on the path of light and honor.

If Islam is the last and most truthful religion, I always have wondered why the fundamentalists and those who truly obey the

Islamic law are so afraid of any other opinion opposed to Islam? Why does any view against Islam appear so dangerous? When the foundation of a religion or an idea is based on truth, there must be no fear of hearing and facing other opinions.

When I speak about fanatic Muslims, I do not mean those who do not practice Islam and the law because they might be even more open to the other ideas and do not mind many changes, but I speak about those who live completely according to the Koran and practice the law every day of their lives.

I intend to discuss the issues which brought up doubts in my mind. These facts are actually my most sincere answers to the question of why I am converted or why did I become a Christian?

"AL ISLAM O HO VAL TASLIM"

"ISLAM MEANS BEING SURRENDERED"

The above-mentioned Arabic verse is actually one of the definitions which explains Islam in a word. "Islam means being surrendered." This verse means that their fanaticism, grudges and false judgments become hindrances to finding out and experiencing the realities of life. According to this verse, man must leave behind all considerations and judgments and just give up and surrender himself completely to Islam.

This is the most common answer to all the questions about law and the lives of prophets: Man is not created to question Allah and the prophets or the law, but he is created to obey and be surrendered.

The Islamic generation began with Ishmael, son of Hajar, whom we can read about in Genesis 16:11-12:

"YOU ARE NOW WITH CHILD AND YOU WILL HAVE A SON. YOU SHALL NAME HIM ISHMAEL, FOR THE LORD HAS HEARD OF YOUR MISERY. HE WILL BE A WILD DONKEY OF A MAN: HIS HAND WILL BE AGAINST EVERY ONE AND EVERY

ONE'S HAND AGAINST HIM, AND HE WILL LIVE IN HOSTILITY TOWARD ALL HIS BROTHERS."

In the year 570 AD, Muhammad was born just like any other ordinary baby. There is no magnificent happening or any extraordinary subject mentioned in his life as a child. He grew up just like any other child and had a completely normal life until he became forty years old. He did not even learn to read and write in his childhood.

So from his birth until he was forty, there was no sign or effect of Muhammad's prophetic mission. Even his uncle Abu Talib who took care of him was unaware of any sign or proof. By the time Muhammad was forty years old, even he himself was unaware of any prophetic mission in his life.

One day when he was in the cave of *Harra*, a stony cavern three kilometers northeast of Mecca, Gabriel appeared to him and said: "Read!"

Muhammad who could not read or write, said: "What shall I read?" and again Gabriel said "Read!" Muhammed repeated: "What shall I read?" and again Gabriel said: "Read!" Muhammad said: "What then shall I read?" Gabriel said:

"READ IN THE NAME OF THY LORD AND CHERISHER WHO CREATED MAN OUT OF A CLOT OF CONGEALED BLOOD...." Sura 96 (AL ALAQ) verses 1-5

After that day when Muhammad took refuge again in the cavern of Harra, neither he received a revelation nor heard a word from Allah; no angel appeared to him again and he was not inspired again by any vision at all.

But that evening in the cavern was actually a beginning for initiating his mission; and it was Khadijeh, Muhammad's first wife—a very wealthy and well-known woman even before her marriage with Muhammad—who assisted him in all aspects, spiritually and financially. There was actually no divine proof of Muhammad's inspiration in the cavern of Harra.

If I intend to explain about the foundation of the Koran, it should be said that the Koran was not written down during Muhammad's life. He did not write down the manuscript of Koran. It was actually left up to his followers to write down whatever Muhammad said.

During the wars in which his followers and Muhammad himself were involved, most of his followers who had memorized Muhammad's revelations got killed or, in other situations, the animals ate the *suras* which were written on the leaves of date-palm or barks of trees and many of the stones and bones which the *suras* were written on were lost and destroyed.

So the historical accounts prove that the Koranic manuscript was destroyed during the years that followed, and it was Abu Bakr, Muhammad's closest friend, who accepted the responsibility to collect the Koran on his own. He ordered the Koranic verses and inserted them in different chapters according to his own thoughts and opinions.

Koran includes 114 chapters and each chapter is called *sura*. Each verse which is marked with a number is called *ayeh*. The collection of the whole chapters and verses of Koran was based on a human's mind, and it is very obvious that human's mind is sensual not divine.

In Islamic faith man must obey the Koran as it is and not question the verses even though the Koran is compiled in a very awkward way and the verses are not in chronological order as Muhammad had received them. Otherwise, first *sura* should be the first revelation that Muhammad received and the last should be the last revelation.

The Koran is put together according to the size of *suras;* as we can see when we read it, it begins with the longest *suras* to the shortest ones at the end of Koran. There are many verses that very clearly show that it is not Allah who speaks but Muhammad himself. Actually in many verses Muhammad expressed an idea first and then he was inspired by verses favorable to his thoughts.

Many verses are repeated because those verses were memorized by mostly illiterate Muslims, and they seem repetitive when literate people read them. Of course, Muslims claim that Muhammad himself repeated some verses many times because Allah knows that men forget soon and so they must be read over and over.

When the Koran is read from the beginning to the end, which I did many times during my Islamic faith, there is always this result that it seems the book has no end. In other words there is no beginning in the Koran and there is no end in the book and the topics of *suras* are quite different from each other. In one *sura* Mohammad fights with his enemies and in another there is advice to Muhammad about his wives and controlling the arguments among them.

In conclusion, there is no divine inspiration to be found in the Koran. One who wishes to be taught by God and divine teachings and receive peace through reading it will not be led through reading the Koranic verses.

Mostly the verses are about fear, hell, darkness, fighting and Allah's threats to man. During my Islamic faith many times I asked these questions, "If the Koran was truly sent by God, why didn't he protect it during the years . . . and if God did not protect that book and it was destroyed, how could Abu Bakr, a man with no divine power, collect it and protect it . . . and if it were sent by God, shouldn't it be devoid of any revenge and negative virtues?"

There is no sign or any miracle which shows that Muhammad was superior to mankind as we read the Koran. When the polytheists asked for a miracle, Muhammad himself answered:

"AM I AUGHT BUT A MAN—A MESSENGER?" sura 17 (Al ISRA) verse 93

Or in another part of verse 94 in the same *sura* we read:

"THEY SAID: HAS ALLAH SENT A MAN [LIKE US] TO BE HIS MESSENGER?"

In order to receive Allah's healing and mercy or to see a miracle from a particular Imam, Muslims tie colored, especially green, pieces of cloth inside the shrines where the Imams' descendants are buried. They throw so much money into the shrines as alms just in hope of seeing a miracle in their lives. There are different shrines and Imam's graves in every city and even in the very small villages.

Some shrines are a lot more famous and some of them are quite unknown but still holy to Muslims. There are those shrines which are obscure, and the one who is buried there is completely unknown with no identity. But Muslims worship all those known and unknown shrines and tombs in a very honorable way with all their hearts.

Muslims tie the green pieces of cloth, put alms and gifts inside the shrines and do all those charities hoping to see a miracle from God and his prophet Muhammad from whom there was absolutely no sign of miracles in his life and even in the holy book that he brought.

When polytheists asked him to perform a miracle, he consistently remained silent or ignored their request. Muhammad himself said that he was a man, a regular man, as we read in *suras* mentioned above.

If Muhammad were just a man according his own claim, just a man like any other regular man, then how could he possibly be inspired by God and receive verses from him?

When the angel appeared to him in the cavern of Harra and told him to read, he was completely illiterate. That miracle happened when he was alone and nobody else was there; but, when people asked him for a miracle in front of their eyes, he said that he was only a man. No one ever saw Muhammad be inspired by verses from God, and there is absolutely no verse in the Koran in confirmation of any miracle by Muhammad.

Actually what Muhammad said was completely correct that he was just a man because his whole life including his birth, his childhood and his innumerable marriages were all exactly like any other man.

According to the Koran Muhammad was asked to perform a miracle by his tribe more than 25 times, but he either remained silent or mentioned that he was just a man.

"AM I AUGHT BUT A MAN—A MESSENGER?"   Sura 17 (AL ISRA) verse 93

God is omnipotent and possesses the infinite power to perform any miracle at any time he determines. Wasn't that a burdensome matter for a man who claimed to be a prophet, not to be able to perform any miracle?

In the Old Testament we read that Moses performed miracles and in the New Testament we see innumerable miracles.

He healed the man born blind in John 9:6:

"WHILE I AM IN THE WORLD, I AM THE LIGHT OF THE WORLD. HAVING SAID THIS, HE SPIT ON THE GROUND, MADE SOME MUD WITH THE SALIVA, AND PUT IT ON THE MAN'S EYES. GO, HE TOLD HIM, WASH IN THE POOL OF SILOAM. SO THE MAN WENT AND WASHED, AND CAME HOME SEEING."

And then again we read in John 6:19-20 how Jesus walked on the water:

"WHEN THEY HAD ROWED THREE OR THREE AND A HALF

MILES, THEY SAW JESUS APPROACHING THE BOAT, WALKING ON THE WATER: AND THEY WERE TERRIFIED. BUT HE SAID TO THEM, IT IS I; DON'T BE AFRAID."

And again we read in John 6:10-11 when he fed five thousand people:

"JESUS SAID, HAVE THE PEOPLE SIT DOWN. THERE WAS PLENTY OF GRASS IN THAT PLACE AND THE MEN SAT DOWN, ABOUT FIVE THOUSAND OF THEM. THEN TOOK THE LOAVES, GAVE THANKS AND DISTRIBUTED TO THOSE WHO WERE SEATED AS MUCH AS THEY WANTED. HE DID THE SAME WITH THE FISH."

And one of the most eminent miracles was when Jesus raised Lazarus from the dead:

"SO THEY TOOK AWAY THE STONE. THEN JESUS LOOKED UP AND SAID, FATHER I THANK YOU THAT YOU HAVE HEARD ME. I KNEW THAT YOU ALWAYS HEAR ME, BUT I SAID THIS FOR THE BENEFIT OF THE PEOPLE STANDING HERE, THAT THEY MAY BELIEVE THAT YOU SENT ME. WHEN HE HAD SAID THIS, JESUS CALLED IN A LOUD VOICE, LAZARUS, COME OUT! THE DEAD MAN CAME OUT, HIS HANDS AND FEET WRAPPED WITH STRIPS OF LINEN AND A CLOTH AROUND HIS FACE." John 11:41-44

And so many other miracles were performed by Jesus Christ

Actually the foundation of Christianity is based on miracles. Jesus' birth, his life and his mission, his death and his resurrection from death were all according to different miracles.

But in Muhammad's life there is no sign of a miracle. He was actually unaware of God's will and was waiting just like other Muslims as we read in *Sura* 10 (Yunus) verse 20:

"THEY SAY: WHY IS NOT A SIGN SENT DOWN TO HIM FROM HIS LORD? SAY: THE UNSEEN IS ONLY FOR ALLAH [TO

KNOW] THEN WAIT YE: I TOO WILL WAIT WITH YOU."

In the Koran the character of Allah is very unknown. He is a terrific and unknown power whose holiness is worshipped. Respecting Allah is the result of man's fear and the question of what happens to me after I die, the result of feeling condemned all the time in the eyes of Allah. And finally the foundation of respecting and obeying Allah is based on fear and being uncertain about future but not love; the relationship with him is actually a one-way relationship.

There are verses found which repeatedly promise hell and threaten to subject man to infernal tortures. In *Sura* 17 (Al Isra) verse 58

"THERE IS NOT A POPULATION BUT WE SHALL DESTROY IT BEFORE THE DAY OF JUDGMENT OR PUNISH IT WITH A DREADFUL PENALTY: THAT IS WRITTEN IN THE [ETERNAL] RECORD."

And also we read in *sura* Alnisa:56 that God is the one who tortures and enjoys when man is tortured and destroyed. God's obstinacy is clearly revealed in that verse. But how can God, whose nature is full of mercy, grace and love, become pleased of burning man in hell?

How can God only promise pain, torture and eternal hell for his creations? How can he who is the omniscient creator of everything perfect and beautiful, who possesses a love and mercy that is world-conquering, have such negative virtues that keep man all the time in fear and alarm?

In the Koran the moral virtues which belong to human nature have been attributed to God: anger, hatred, contentment, indignation and even being cunning. God's justice is presented in the most dreadful way and infernal torture is promised for infidels and all those who have denied Islam and his prophet in *Sura* 33 (Al Ahzab) verse 61:

"THEY SHALL HAVE A CURSE ON THEM: WHEREVER THEY ARE FOUND, THEY SHALL BE SEIZED AND SLAIN [WITHOUT MERCY]."

Sura 9 (Al Tawbah) verse 29:

"SLAY THOSE WHO BELIEVE NOT IN ALLAH NOR THE LAST DAY."

Sura 22 (Al Hajj) verse 39:

"TO THOSE AGAINST WHOM WAR IS MADE, PERMISSION IS GIVEN [TO SLAY], BECAUSE THEY ARE WRONGED AND VERILY, ALLAH IS MOST POWERFUL FOR THEIR AID."

Sura 9 (Al Tawbah) verse 29:

"SLAY THOSE WHO BELIEVE NOT IN ALLAH NOR THE LAST DAY, NOR HOLD THAT FORBIDDEN WHICH HATH FORBIDDEN BY ALLAH AND HIS MESSENGER, NOT ACKNOWLEDGE THE RELIGION OF TRUTH, FROM AMONG THE PEOPLE OF THE BOOK, UNTIL THEY PAY THE JAZYAH [TRIBUTE] WITH WILLING SUBMISSION, AND FEEL THEMSELVES SUBDUED."

Sura 9 (Al Tawbeh) verse 73:

"O PROPHET! STRIVE HARD AGAINST THE UNBELIEVERS AND THE HYPOCRITES AND BE FIRM AGAINST THEM. THEIR ABODE IS HELL AND EVIL REFUGE INDEED."

When there is power and miracles can be performed, torture and law by the sword is not needed. Muhammed fought and revenged his enemies many years of his life. How can a man of God, someone who claimed he had been sent by God, fight constantly and revenge his enemies? How can someone sent by God hold divine verses in one hand and a sword in the other hand?

Twelve years after Muhammad started his mission and when his sword began to shine, even polytheists, who God had said would not believe even if they see the angels, accepted Islam—not by their choice but out of force and fear. There is truly no relationship between light and darkness.

As we read in the Bible in James 3:11:

"CAN BOTH FRESH WATER AND SALT WATER FLOW FROM THE SAME SPRING?"

Or in another chapter in 2 Corinthians 6:14 we read:

"DO NOT BE YOKED TOGETHER WITH UNBELIEVERS, FOR WHAT DO RIGHTEOUSNESS AND WICKEDNESS HAVE IN COMMON? OR WHAT FELLOWSHIP CAN LIGHT HAVE WITH DARKNESS?"

Arabic is the official language of Islam and the Koran. All the prayers and especially *Namaz* must be done in Arabic. In order to worship Allah, the Koran must be read in Arabic and not any other language. Of course, there are different translations of the Koran which can be read in order to obtain information about Koranic verses; but to worship Allah the book must be read in Arabic.

Why must I as an Iranian whose mother language is Persian perform my daily prayers, the *Namaz*, in the Arabic language—a language that my grandparents and my generation have not spoken . . . a language that I do not even understand the meanings of the whole prayers and the verses in Koran. Why should I take my prayers in front of God in a foreign language?

Does Almighty God who has created everything with so much delicacy and care and has all the power on the earth and in the sky only understand Arabic? Many times I asked Allah why I had to use Arabic as a credit in front of him. I believed that Allah is a racist power who understands only Arabic. Many times I asked what happened to all that power that Allah has if he does not understand and does not accept my prayers in Persian!! And performing seventeen times prayers a day!!!

Namaz is one of the most important rules in Islam. It is every

Muslim's duty to perform the *Namaz*. The way of performing *Namaz* has been cleared through tradition. There is no strict written order in the Koran about how it must be performed. A Muslim's prayer must be performed towards Mecca (Kiblan, the direction to which Muhammad turned in prayer). Muslims must pray seventeen times a day before Allah which must be done in certain times and only in the Arabic language.

I have always asked this question that God can hear our prayers only in those certain times? Doesn't God understand the prayer if man is not standing towards Mecca? Does God really need that seventeen times in a day we bow down and beg him for forgiveness? Does he only understand Arabic? If he is so mighty and able to do anything in any moment, how come he does not understand one simple language which is my mother language? What happened to all his wisdom, power, and divinity?

I am Iranian and my mother language is Persian. Why do I have to pray in a foreign language that I do not understand?

Isn't that racism when all the prayers must be done only in Arabic? When I was Muslim I came to that conclusion that Allah is only able to understand Arabic. Performing *Namaz* must be in Arabic, reading Koran must be in Arabic and so as all the prayers. I, as a Muslim, had to think like Arabs and follow their styles of worship if I wanted to be accepted by Allah. Actually the whole religion and the law emphasize the Arabic language and Arabic style of living.

Muslims fast one month of the year (which is called *Ramadan*). Many Muslims who even do not obey the law during the year and do not practice their *Namaz* or probably even drink alcohol, try to be good Muslims and fast during *Ramadan*. Women who usually do not wear veil, try to have veil during *Ramadan;* they do not even shake hands with those who are not intimate ones. They all try to fast during *Ramadan,* but when the month is over, they go back to their normal life until the next *Ramadan.*

What I intend to explain is that God's character in Islam is presented in a way that he can be bought by our good deeds. He will be satisfied by what we do.

Performing *Namaz,* fasting, helping the poor and all the charitable deeds are done in order to buy God and his satisfaction. Allah might observe those good deeds, do a favor and ignore the indecent human's acts. Man tries to cover and hide his sins through and by his good deeds.

RULE OF JIHAD

Holy war, *Jihad,* is the roughest rule in Islam. We cannot see any rule like that in other religions. That rule is only found in Islam—a rule which was pronounced on the basis of strategies and the Islamic conquerers. Muhammed led the battle of *Badr,* one of the most famous battles, in which he gained the *Meccan* leadership as the result of his victory because of superior military strategy and many well-trained zealous followers. There was also the battle of *Uhud* where, although he was defeated, he continued and tried harder than ever to strengthen his position and power, and it was actually through that rule that he established a powerful Islamic government.

I have always wanted to follow and obey the one who is sinless . . . one who had a pure life and never fought. How can someone who has sinned himself be a leader for others? Muhammad sinned and, in *Sura* 40 (Ghafir) verse 55, we read that God demanded Muhammed to ask for forgiveness:

"PATIENTLY, THEN, PERSEVERE: FOR THE PROMISE OF ALLAH IS TRUE: AND ASK FORGIVENESS FOR THY FAULT, AND CELEBRATE THE PRAISES OF THY LORD IN THE EVENING AND

IN THE MORNING."

Muhammad lived and got married just like any other regular man as he himself claimed in *Sura* 17 (AL Isra) verse 93:

"AM I AUGHT BUT A MAN—A MESSENGER?"

Muhammad's birth, his life, his numerous marriages and his death were like any other regular man. During his mission he fought to gain power and when he died, he remained in his grave forever.

Even in Koran *Sura* 10 (yunus) verse 95, we read that God punished Muhammad for his sensual desires when he was out of control:

"NOR BE OF THOSE WHO REJECT THE SIGNS OF ALLAH, OR THOU SHALT BE OF THOSE WHO PERISH."

When a child is born in a Muslim family, especially the fanatic families, according to the law in Koran the child must remain Muslim for the rest of his life. NO MUSLIM IS ALLOWED TO CONVERT. THE CONVERTED MUSLIMS WHO DENY ISLAM ARE WORTHY OF DEATH.

A Muslim born is condemned to remain Muslim all his life. There are those converted Muslims who got killed for their Christian faith according to Islamic law. No Muslim is allowed to deny Islam; otherwise he is an infidel, *kafar,* and must be slain according to Islamic law. There are many verses in the Koran which confirm and support slaying the deniers, *mortad.*

Sura 2 (Al Baqarah) verse 246:

"IF YE WERE COMMANDED TO SLAY, THAT YE WILL NOT FIGHT? THEY SAID: HOW COULD WE REFUSE TO FIGHT IN THE CAUSE OF ALLAH?"

Sura 3 (Al Imran) verse 85:

"IF ANYONE DESIRES A RELIGION OTHER THAN ISLAM

[SUBMISSION TO ALLAH, NEVER WILL IT BE ACCEPTED OF HIM.]"

And there are still more verses which confirm what the Islamic law says:

ALL THE DENIERS [MORTAD, KAFAR] MUST EITHER DIE OR TURN FROM THEIR APOSTASY AND REPENT IN THE NAME OF ALLAH AND MUHAMMAD.

MY POSITION AS A WOMAN IN ISLAM

Sura 4 (Al Nisa) verse 34:

"MEN ARE THE PROTECTORS AND MAINTAINERS OF WOMEN BECAUSE ALLAH HAS GIVEN THE ONE MORE [STRENGTH] THAN THE OTHER."

In Islam not only is equality of men and women not found, but also men are superior and are rulers of women's existence. According to law women are weak creatures. A woman inherits half of man and her right in witnessing is half of man. It is the men who have the right of divorce and—according to law—prophecy, religious leadership, public homily and call to prayer is just for men. Men are actually gifted with wisdom and prudence according to the Koran. They are stronger than women and they actually own women when they marry them.

Jockying, shooting, witnessing for performance of Islamic law and so many other possibilities are just for men. Women are in a lower level of life. Beating women is permissible, and there are actually verses in the Koran which recommend beating women.

Sura 4 (Al Nisa) verse 34:

"AS TO THOSE WOMEN ON WHOSE PART YE FEAR DISLOY-ALTY AND ILL-CONDUCT, ADMONISH THEM [FIRST], [NEXT], REFUSE TO SHARE THEIR BEDS, [AND LAST] BEAT THEM [LIGHTLY]."

Marriage is on the basis of different contracts in Islamic law—permanent or temporary with a short- or long-marriage contract. A man can conclude a temporary marriage contract with a woman even for a few days and, according to law, their contract would be canceled on the specified day. Polygamy is allowed and a man can be married with several women at the same time permanently or temporarily.

During the years that I studied the Koran with my private teacher, there was always a verse which I thought was the most humiliating for me as a woman. Even during the years when I still had no doubt about my Islamic faith, it always brought a big question mark to my mind.

Sura 2 (Al Baqarah) verse 223:

"YOUR WIVES ARE AS A TILTH UNTO YOU SO APPROACH YOUR TILTH WHEN OR HOW YOU WILL."

Muhammad had numerous marriages. Khadijeh, a very wealthy woman, was his first wife, and his youngest wife was Ayeshe who was only seven years old when Muhammad approached her family about the marriage.

How could a prophet who claimed he is a prominent prophet marry a seven-year-old child? Because Ayeshe was so young and needed more time to grow, Muhammad had to wait two years for her to grow. During the time of waiting, he married Sudeh and, at the same time, prepared himself for marriage with Ayeshe. By the time he married Ayeshe, he was forty years old and Ayeshe was only nine years old. Muhammad had about twenty wives in his sanctuary at the same time.

There are verses in the Koran which confirm and support Muhammad's numerous marriages and his relationships among his wives.

Sura 33 (Al Ahzab) verse 50:

"O PROPHET! WE HAVE MADE LAWFUL TO THEE THY WIVES TO WHOM THOU HAST PAID THEIR SOWERS AND THOSE WHOM THY RIGHT HAND POSSESSES OUT OF THE PRISONERS OF WAR WHOM ALLAH HAS ASSIGNED TO THEE AND DAUGHTERS OF THY PATERNAL UNCLES AND AUNTS AND DAUGHTERS OF THY MATERNAL UNCLES AND AUNTS WHO MIGRATED [FROM MECCA] WITH THEE AND ANY BELIEVING WOMAN WHO DEDICATES HER SOUL TO THE PROPHET IF THE PROPHET WISHES TO WED HE. THIS ONLY FOR THEE AND NOT FOR THE BELIEVERS [AT LARGE]. WE KNOW WHAT WE HAVE APPOINTED FOR THEM AS TO THEIR WIVES AND THE CAPTIVES WHOM THEIR RIGHT HANDS POSSESS—IN ORDER THAT THERE SHOULD BE NO DIFFICULTY FOR THEE. AND ALLAH IS FORGIVING. MOST MERCIFUL."

And then in another verse when Muhammad's marriages got out of control, God prohibited him of marrying more women.

Sura 33 (Al Ahzab) verse 52:

"IT IS NOT LAWFUL FOR THEE [TO MARRY MORE] WOMEN AFTER THIS, NOR TO CHANGE THEM FOR [OTHER] WIVES, EVEN THOUGH THEIR BEAUTY ATTRACTS THEE, EXCEPT ANY THY RIGHT HAND SHOULD POSSESS [AS HANDMAIDENS] AND ALLAH DOTH WATCH OVER ALL THINGS."

I have always wanted to follow the one who has been free from all worldly anxieties, the one who has been pure from this world and its desires, the one whose birth has been unique, the one who I can go to whenever I need him and pray in my own mother language; and, finally, the one who does not bring fear to me by law and does not judge me all the time.

God's character in Islam is presented as a subduer, God of condemnation, contempt, easy anger, and eager to be worshipped.

God does not need that we perform the ablution ceremony

five times a day and perform *Namaz* seventeen times a day—two prayer rounds in the early morning, four times noontime prayer, four times mid-afternoon prayer, three times sunset prayer and four times the evening prayer. He does not need our fasting just in order to accomplish one rule. He wants us to become pure from inside and become united with him. He wants to take away the distance which is created between himself and us.

Islam was established on the basis of power and conquest. Muhammad fought in many wars during his life and he died among his numerous wives when he was sixty-three years old. He did not declare any successor when he died and did not make any decisions for the future of Muslims and the Islamic government; therefore, many discussions and decisions were made after his death.

Even the Koran, which was the only evidence of Muhammad's mission and his instructions, was compiled after his death—evidence which is collected in many verses which promise just pain and hell and killing the infidels and deniers.

Sura 4 (Al Nisa) verse 91:

"IF THEY WITHDRAW NOT FROM YOU NOR GIVE YOU GUARANTEES OF PEACE BESIDES RESTRAINING THEIR HAND, SEIZE THEM AND SLAY THEM WHEREVER YE GET THEM, IN THEIR CASE WE HAVE PROVIDED YOU WITH A CLEAR ARGUMENT AGAINST THEM."

The day that I chose Jesus Christ as a savior in my life was the day that I decided to follow and obey the one who is filled with God's spirit. Even in the Koran it is written in *Sura* 19 (Maryam) verse 17.

I had always wanted to follow the one whose birth was unique. Matthew 1:23: "The virgin will be with child and will give birth to a son, and they will call him Immanuel," which means "God with us."

Jesus was a birth which happened as a miracle not like thousands of newborn babies. I decided to follow Christ because he never fought and killed others for power, he did not conquer anybody or any place by force. He did not have any worldly desire in his life. He did not even get married while the other prophets married so many different women, and most importantly of all, he never revenged anybody but forgave.

The time that he was on the cross and under the pain of the whole world, he still said, "Father forgive them."

"JESUS SAID, FATHER FORGIVE THEM, FOR THEY DO NOT KNOW WHAT THEY ARE DOING." Luke 23:34

His life was full of miracles in all aspects and finally the greatest miracle and event which happened on the cross. He died on the cross and they put him in the grave, but he did not remain in grave and was resurrected after three days—while everybody else, even the prophets, all remained in their graves forever after their death.

I WANT TO WORSHIP A LIVING GOD WHO HEARS MY PRAYERS ANY TIME AND ANYWHERE . . . A LIVING GOD WHO ROSE FROM THE DEAD AND SINCE THEN HIS TOMB HAS REMAINED EMPTY.

THE TOMB IS EMPTY

Yes, his tomb is empty while everybody else, including all the prophets, have remained in their graves forever after their deaths. PRAISE THE LORD FOR HIS EMPTY TOMB! His empty tomb is actually the main reason that his living word is being spread so fast around the world and people from every nationality and every country and nation give their hearts to Christ's name.

JESUS CHRIST'S resurrection is the result of a perfect victory and love. By accepting Jesus in my heart, I had gotten to the spring of light and peace. I started to know God in a new way.

Christianity is not just a religion but a relationship, and Jesus does not introduce himself as a prophet who was sent by God.

Jesus performed so many great miracles that the history of man does not remember anyone else who has been able to do so. He actually changed the whole history with his mission, and His birth became the beginning of the history of the world. He did not conquer with military might, and he never held a sword in his hand. He never imposed himself and he never fought to obtain victory and he did not compile any laws. He was a power who did not sit in a palace while others fought for him in order to obtain power. He went among people—not fighting or imposing his own thoughts—but carrying the burdens of mankind.

Matthew 11: 28-30:

"COME TO ME, ALL YOU WHO ARE WEARY AND BUR-
DENED, AND I WILL GIVE YOU REST. TAKE MY YOKE UPON
YOU AND LEARN FROM ME, FOR I AM GENTLE AND HUMBLE
IN HEART, AND YOU WILL FIND REST FOR YOUR SOULS. FOR
MY YOKE IS EASY AND MY BURDEN IS LIGHT."

Which power is greater? The one who sits in his palace and
people must go and beg him for mercy and forgiveness or the one
who goes among people and serves them and sacrifices himself
for them?

All this requires a super human power which is God's power.
As Jesus said:

"ANYONE WHO HAS SEEN ME HAS SEEN THE FATHER."
John 14:9

Jesus says: "HERE I AM! I STAND AT THE DOOR AND
KNOCK. IF ANYONE HEARS MY VOICE AND OPENS THE DOOR,
I WILL COME IN AND EAT WITH HIM, AND HE WITH ME."
Revelation 3:20

Actually becoming a follower of Christ is becoming a follower of his peace and a follower of his victories—great victories that
he creates in us and in our life if we trust him.

But in my Islamic faith I had to run after different doors and
beg one of them to open for me. I actually came to the conclusion that in Islam all the doors were closed and man remains
behind the closed doors forever.

I was fascinated by how Jesus healed the sick. I was more fascinated when I understood that anyone who believes in his name
can do the same: "IF YOU HAVE FAITH AS SMALL AS A MUS-
TARD SEED, YOU CAN SAY TO THIS MOUNTAIN, MOVE FROM
HERE TO THERE AND IT WILL MOVE."   Matthew 17:20

Jesus never gave slogans but fulfilled all his promises. He performed whatever he preached. He said nothing which was not truth. When he said the blind will see, and the lame will walk, the miracles did happen.

"THEN WILL THE EYES OF THE BLIND BE OPENED AND THE EARS OF THE DEAF UNSTOPPED. THEN WILL THE LAME LEAP LIKE A DEER, AND THE MUTE TONGUE SHOUT FOR JOY." Isaiah 35: 5-6

There is no way to create trust by force or to create love by mendacity. Jesus Christ is the only power who heals the broken and branded heart.

God's kingdom is actually finding the lost sheep.

Luke 15:4-6:

"SUPPOSE ONE OF YOU HAS A HUNDRED SHEEP AND LOSES ONE OF THEM. DOES HE NOT LEAVE THE NINETY-NINE IN THE OPEN COUNTRY AND GO AFTER THE LOST SHEEP UNTIL HE FINDS IT? AND WHEN HE FINDS IT HE JOYFULLY PUTS IT ON HIS SHOULDERS AND GOES HOME. THEN HE CALLS HIS FRIENDS AND NEIGHBORS TOGETHER AND SAYS REJOICE WITH ME I HAVE FOUND MY LOST SHEEP."

God's kingdom is returning of the lost son.

Luke 15:31-32:

"MY SON THE FATHER SAID YOU ARE ALWAYS WITH ME AND EVERY THING I HAVE IS YOURS. BUT WE HAD TO CELEBRATE AND BE GLAD BECAUSE THIS BROTHER OF YOURS WAS DEAD AND HE IS ALIVE AGAIN: HE WAS LOST AND IS FOUND."

Even in the Koran which Muslims believe, it is the supreme revelation of God, Jesus Christ has been represented as the greatest power who raised the dead.

In *Sura* 36 (Ya Sin) verse 12, it is written that only God can raise the dead; and in *Sura* 5 (Al Maidah) verse 110, it is written that Jesus was the only one who had that power. So even the

Koran shows that Jesus Christ is a perfect image of God.

We begin our spiritual life with trusting and resting in Jesus Christ and that will always be the source of power for our steady and unstumbling way.

All mankind from any race or color, man or woman, are God's poetry in creation. In Islam people try to hide their sins through their good deeds. No matter how hard I prayed and obeyed the Islamic law, I never succeeded in reaching God and I never heard him because my sins were those hindrances between God and me.

Jesus Christ washes away all the sins like a roaring river and he is the bridge from a world of ignorance and darkness to the wonderful and restful world of light and hope. After crossing that bridge, I knew where I was going and I felt his touch on my life. HALLELUJAH! Jesus Christ had shaken the rocks of my life.

Before I used to go and knock on doors where nobody was inside to open them, but it was only Jesus Christ who said in Revelation 3:20:

"HERE I AM! I STAND AT THE DOOR AND KNOCK. IF ANY-ONE HEARS MY VOICE AND OPENS THE DOOR, I WILL COME IN AND EAT WITH HIM, AND HE WITH ME."

Jesus Christ pounds on the door which has no bell and knocks on the door which has no knocker and enters. Living without Christ is a risk, but with him life is full of wonderful surprises.

In conformity with the necessities of this world, my life is only a drop in the ocean which shows only a small piece of Christ's vast power and love. Love is the way of his kingdom, a pure love that will never be broken:

"LOVE IS PATIENT, LOVE IS KIND. IT DOESN'T ENVY, IT DOESN'T BOAST, IT IS NOT PROUD. IT IS NOT RUDE, IT IS NOT

SELF-SEEKING, IT IS NOT EASILY ANGERED. IT KEEPS NO RECORD OF WRONGS. LOVE DOES NOT DELIGHT IN EVIL BUT REJOICES WITH TRUTH. IT ALWAYS PROTECTS, ALWAYS TRUSTS, ALWAYS HOPES, ALWAYS PRESERVES."   1 Corinthians 13:4-7

In the name of Christ, I have learned to live the life which Jesus Christ has given me one more time. I want to see the life and feel it and understand what the world is really about rather than reading about it. I know that greatness must be in my look not in what I am looking at. Now I know who I am and where I am going. I have learned to move on rather than to wait and concentrate on what will happen if I do not go. Today God has called us towards himself and he has called us his children. Let us be filled with his spirit and his peace and let us live with him every day of our life so that all the victories that he had in his spirit would be transferred to us.

I cannot give up but want every day to be more available for the Lord to use me in his wonderful and marvelous ways. After my last journey from Iran, having passed through the ups and downs of the storms of life, I have cast anchor in my Lord, rolled up my sail, put away my oars, and let go of the rudder. I have come to the harbor and thrown myself into the arms of my Lord where I feel the firmness and security of the Lord in my steps.

WHY DO I LIVE?

There always have been three kinds of honest feelings taking over my life: loving and honoring God, doing research in human social affairs, and sadness concerning human calamities. These three feelings have drawn me constantly to here and there just like severe hurricanes and amazing storms.

Sometimes the Holy Spirit has increased my joy so much that I am taken to the heavens, and sometimes the sorrows of mankind have taken me to the depths of the deepest ocean and have thrown me to the extremes of despair and hopelessness.

I have been consistently after the truth of God for these reasons:

The presence of the Lord brings the good news of joy and freshness in man's heart and life—such joy that I have sacrificed the rest of my life to gain more of that joy and rest. He always has taken away my loneliness . . . a fearful loneliness which brings man to the point of trembling by its blackness and its silence and changes man's world to a cold and lifeless abyss where the only solution for man is to be released from there and refuge in the Lord and his greatness. And, finally, because I have always been a searcher for truth, I saw these truths only in the unity which has been established between God and man.

Searching for truth has always been my goal in life, although searching and going after truth sometimes creates troubles and dangerous ups and downs and even might threaten life to death for that truth.

It has always been my deep desire to search about social life of man and man's morals. It has always been my prayer to be able to perceive man's heart. I always have had the desire to understand why the stars shine in some people's hearts while the sparkle in other hearts has been extinguished. I want to learn more about the lack of seriousness of man's heart.

People go to therapy classes and different gatherings in order to find a healthy spirit, to find out who they are. They try to get help from anything they can to perform self-revelation. There are selfish beings within man from which it is impossible to separate by one's own power—just like charcoal and fire which seem to be two different things, but fire is always hidden in the heart of charcoal.

Mankind is so sick that until one has discovered his inner being, he cannot know even himself. The Dead Sea is the only sea where there is no sign of life. Every living thing dies in that sea because it has nothing to give but destruction. Man's inner being is exactly like that sea if he does not find out who he is and why he has come into this world.

Picturing the faces of those who stood for Christ and died for his name, picturing their faces as they breathed their last moments of life brings pain to my heart. The entreating looks of those who are driven away from their homeland, when they escape and look for a refuge for continuing their lives creates a deep pain in me. I have always wished to weaken the evil forces through my faith and in the name of my Lord JESUS CHRIST. We all suffer iniquities, but which of us can destroy the dark forces by our own power?

I have resorted to my Lord Christ in my life in order to be able to strike a blow against wickedness and all the darkness of life in the powerful name of Jesus Christ. To become a Christian is not simply changing a religion or accepting an historical event because Christianity is not merely a religion and what Christ did is not just an historical event. When I gave my heart to Christ, my whole being was changed and I actually was born one more time in my soul and my spirit.

This is the way of my life and I will continue this way as long as I still have life.

I walk through light.
I see the light of life along by the streams and pathways
    and even through the trees.
I croon the songs of victory which pass gently in my mind.
I am in the beginning of the way.
During my steps in storm and snow and the heat of the years,
    the memorable nights of summer and cold storms of
    winter burned under sunshine and overflowed with God's
    blessings.
I feel my steps that I am on the right road.
The road which goes to light and truth.

My past memories sound like bells from afar. The sweet melodies of my childhood, the intoxicating spring fresh weather during new year *(Nourooz)*, those beautiful gardens along the blue lakes and the heart-ravishing sunsets, sitting under the sunshine in the days of winter towards the mountains which were covered with snow, waiting to hear something new, my very first prayer in my Lord's name and leaving behind the dark world of law and all its sanctities devoid of truth.

Now, that childish happiness is gone and a new eagerness that I can show to others is established inside me. How much my joy in the Lord gives me peace and rest!

There is no winter in my heart anymore. Whatever there is found is summer. Experiencing dark and strange places make me feel bad. No longer do I throw my hat into the air simply and no longer do I sing the Lord's songs without any reason.

I smile—not with my lips—but with my spirit, with my eyes and with my whole being. Today life crowds me with all its beauties. Christ has given a new meaning to my life, a meaning which is completely different from before, new meanings which are more delicate, more quiet, more experienced, more grateful and overflowing with peace and rest and full of his victories.

From the day that I went to Christ, everything has been more meaningful to me more than before, and life has spoken to me in a richer and more peaceful language.

My wishes do not paint the secret distances with dreamy colors any more and my eyes are convinced and satisfied to see what exists and to see all the realities of life and existence because I have taught my eyes to see.

The whole world has become more beautiful than before.

I never suffer loneliness anymore because Christ started to live within me. I do not want my life to be anything else than it is right now even though I die in the way that I have started.

I am ready to remain under the sun of life so long that I develop gradually and become experienced completely. In this period of life, I have a great desire to become more perfect, more complete. I desire evolution.

I am one of those who are goers in life not one of the ones who remain. I am a new creation in Christ, a newborn Christian who has learned to transfer to others what the Lord whispered to me until others also find that spiritual birth that I found and I will, through word and deed, share and transfer what I have found to others through faith and in the powerful name of my Lord Jesus Christ.

AFTERWORD

Our impulsive escape from my homeland and being away for many years from home in foreign lands—with its ups and downs and permanent rejection by my fundamentalist family—not only did not make me give up but also made me more experienced and more mature in my Christian faith.

The day I left Iran, I thought I was released from the hands of dark and fanatic forces. Through my immigration to the north of Europe, I thought I had found a safe place where I could continue my life and serve my Lord in tranquility. Unfortunately the seal of rejection not only has been sealed on my name in my father's identity card but also on the files and minds of fanatic forces.

I thought we could settle down in the north of Europe and continuously pray for the day the Lord opens the doors of Iran through his miraculous ways—the day that Iranian converted Muslims would be free to go back to Iran.

But after a few years of life and serving the Lord in different churches and Christian organizations in the north of Europe, the fanatic forces started to attack and put me under so much pressure that again for the safety of my life, I had to leave there. I went to the United States in the belief that my life would perhaps be more secure.

I believe that God teaches his most perfect and beautiful lessons and plans right in the middle of calamities and troubles. That is the reason I have learned never to give up.

For security reasons I content myself to describe this much about my past year, although I might not be safe even in this country. I continue to walk with Christ firmly, and it is my daily prayer with all my brothers and sisters who are united in this prayer that the Lord will open the doors of Iran and the church of Iran would grow stronger than ever.

Until that day we will hold our Bibles in our hands, stand firm in the powerful name of Jesus Christ and with united shouts of HALLELUJAH! shake the world of darkness and look at life exactly the way that Jesus Christ, our Lord, looked.

*To order additional copies of this book
or to learn more about
ministry among Muslims,
please contact the following:*

Don't Keep Me Silent
P.O. Box 4331
Silver Spring, MD 20914-4331